BLUE UPRIGHT

BOOKS BY STEVE RAYMOND

Kamloops: An Angler's Study of the Kamloops Trout

The Year of the Angler

The Year of the Trout

Backcasts: A History of the Washington Fly Fishing Club, 1939-1989

Steelhead Country

The Estuary Flyfisher

Rivers of the Heart

Blue Upright

BLUE UPRIGHT

THE FLIES OF A LIFETIME

Steve Raymond

Illustrations by
August C. Kristoferson

Skyhorse Publishing

Visit our website at www.skyhorsepublishing.com.

10 9 8 7 6 5 4 3 2 1

Library of Congress Cataloging-in-Publication Data is available on file.

Cover design by Stephanie Doyle

Print ISBN: 978-1-63220-516-2
Ebook ISBN: 978-1-63220-894-1

Printed in the United States of America

for Aileen

who caught her first fish June 21, 2002
(with a little help from her grandpa)

Special thanks to Richard B. (Dick) Thompson of Ellensburg, Washington, for relating the history of the TDC fly pattern, to Jerry Doak of Doaktown, New Brunswick, for sharing the results of his research into the history of the Green Machine, and to August C. "Kris" Kristoferson, whose illustrations of my flies look better than the real thing.

CONTENTS

PREFACE

IMITATION IS THE SINCEREST FORM of fly fishing. To take fur, feathers or synthetic materials, each lifeless and inanimate by itself, and blend them together to create the image of a living insect is doubtless art in one of its highest forms. It requires imagination and skill, creativity and discipline, patience and vision.

As in other kinds of art, some people excel at this. I admit readily that I am not one of them. For several reasons, including lack of patience, proper training and manual dexterity, the flies that emerge from my vise have never been the sort worth framing and hanging on the wall. But I don't tie flies for that purpose; I tie them because it gives me pleasure and because I need them to catch fish.

I live in a house full of flies: Flies for trout and steelhead, flies for Atlantic and Pacific salmon, flies for bonefish and other saltwater species, flies for rivers, lakes, beaver ponds, estuaries and the open sea. I have flies framed on the walls, flies in boxes of all kinds, flies in paintings and photographs, and flies stuck in the lamb's wool patches of several fishing vests hanging in my closet. The best ones—those in the frames and photographs—are the work of other tyers whose capabilities far exceed my own. The rest are mostly flies I tied myself, for fishing. When I contemplate their number and variety, I am astounded at the enormous investment of time they represent, exceeded only by the amount of time I have actually spent fishing them. Together, these activities—tying flies and fishing them—account for a major portion of my life. I am fortunate, for I cannot think of a better way to have spent the time.

I taught myself to tie flies, undoubtedly the main reason my dressings have never achieved artistic quality. My only sources of help were a couple of old books that were already badly out of date by the time I read them. As a result, the techniques I learned were obsolete and the habits I developed were grossly inefficient. By the time I realized this it was too late to do anything about it; when I tried to learn modern methods and the use of modern tools, it was more difficult than trying to start all over again. My old methods and habits were ingrained too deeply to be changed, so I still tie flies the way I always have.

The result is that the products of my tying vise are no closer now to perfection than they ever have been. No matter how diligently I try to make them right, my flies always turn out a little off center, a little out of proportion, or with stray hackle fibers sticking out where they don't belong. Sometimes they come unraveled while I'm casting, and when I retrieve the fly I'll discover it's missing some vital piece or part.

Despite all these shortcomings, I still greatly enjoy the experience of tying flies—and fishing them. Fortunately, the imperfections of my patterns have never been a deterrent to the fish I seek. Trout, steelhead, bonefish, salmon and other species have always responded well to my slightly cockeyed patterns, and it's their approval that really counts.

The fly patterns in this book are among those that have served me most faithfully over the years, the favorite flies of a long angling life. A few are widely known; their names will be instantly recognizable to anglers everywhere. A few others are relatively unknown outside the Pacific Northwest, where I live and do most of my fishing; perhaps this book will help them gain wider appreciation. Others are my own patterns, which I use alone or share with a few fishing friends. It is not my purpose to urge them upon a wider audience; rather, I hope they might stimulate ideas in the minds of other tyers, notions they can incorporate in their own dressings or adapt for use on their own waters.

For me, these flies also are objects of treasured memory. Each time I open a fly box and see an old Carey Special, a battered Skunk, or a beat-up Salmon Candy, it reminds me of familiar faces and favorite places, of incidents funny or sad, of memorable fish and memorable days of fishing. Sometimes the colors of the flies have faded, but they still evoke vivid images of anglers who have passed through my life, of things they said or did, of time we spent together on the water. All this history, and more, is somehow bound up in the combination of fur, feather, tinsel and thread wrapped around the shank of each hook.

If a fly is supposed to represent life, then these flies represent the memories of my fishing life. Now it is my pleasure to share some of these flies and some of those memories with you.

—*Steve Raymond*
Clinton, Washington

1
CAREY SPECIAL

Hook: No. 4-8
Thread: Black or olive
Tail: None
Body: Olive chenille
Hackle: Two or three turns of brown pheasant rump
(One of many modern versions)

COLONEL CAREY WAS FRUSTRATED. The Kamloops trout in Arthur Lake were feeding avidly on dragonfly nymphs, but when the Colonel looked through his fly assortment he could not find a good imitation.

Fortunately, the Colonel—some say his first name was Tom, but he is now almost universally remembered by his British Army rank—had remembered to bring his fly-tying gear. After giving the matter some thought, he clamped a No. 6 hook in his vise and began to fashion a new pattern intended to match the appearance of the dragonfly nymphs emerging from the little-known southern British Columbia lake where he was camped.

For the tail and body of the fly he selected ground-hog (marmot) hair. This was not a surprising choice for the time and place; ground hogs were considered a local nuisance for their habit of burrowing under log cabins and keeping the occupants awake at night. The occupants dealt with the problem in a variety of ways, all spelling bad news for the ground hogs, so ground-hog hair was in plentiful supply.

The Colonel twisted the hair around the hook shank, bound it in place with black linen thread and trimmed away the stray fibers. The result was a round, bulky, mottled body that, to the Colonel's eye, was a good representation of the body of a natural dragonfly nymph.

The next step was to find the right hackle. This was necessary not only to give the fly an illusion of movement in the water, but also because the fly-tying conventions of the time demanded that every fly should have hackle, and Colonel Carey was not about to defy convention. He may have experimented with several different alternatives before settling on his final choice, the rump feather from a mature Chinese pheasant rooster. Not content with only one of these, he decided the fly should have two.

The Colonel's choice of pheasant rump might have been influenced by his familiarity with another fly already in use on some of British Columbia's Kamloops trout lakes. This pattern, known as the Pazooka (later much more widely known as the Knouff Special), also had a pheasant rump hackle. But regardless of the source of the idea, Colonel Carey hardly could have made a better choice; nature might have created the rump feather of a mature Chinese pheasant rooster specifically with fly tyers in mind. It is a large, oval-shaped, mottled gray-green feather with tints of brown, black and sometimes yellow in its center, and its long, slender fibers taper gracefully to narrow tips. When fastened about a hook and bound properly, these fibers sweep backward and provide lifelike pulses of movement when the fly is retrieved through the water.

By choosing a pair of these feathers and tying them very full, Colonel Carey added bulk to his fly—necessary to imitate the stout, stubby shape of a mature dragonfly nymph—and simultaneously assured that the fly would have good movement in the water.

History does not record the precise date of Colonel Carey's invention; we know only that it happened early in the 1930s. Neither is there any record of the results he achieved with his new fly, but we may infer they were good because within a very few years the pattern was being fished widely throughout British Columbia. By then it had become known by several different names, including "The Dredge" and the "Monkey-Faced Louise," but as its popularity spread it eventually became known as the Carey Special in honor of its creator. By that name it survives and thrives today.

IN THE DECADES SINCE ITS CREATION, the Carey Special has evolved from a specific dressing into a generic style of tying. Now there exist countless versions, though all still bear the name Carey Special. The use of pheasant rump for the hackle is just about the only feature of the original pattern that remains in all the modern variations, though even that has changed; while Colonel Carey used a pair of feathers and tied them very full in the original, the fly now is most often tied sparsely with a single feather. In contemporary fly-tying parlance it would be considered a "soft-hackle" pattern.

Nobody uses ground-hog hair for the body any more, and the pattern now is most often dressed with a body of chenille, floss or any number of synthetic materials. Tied with a stout body of dark olive or brown, the Carey Special still makes an excellent dragonfly nymph imitation. With a slender body of the same colors, it serves equally well as an imitation of a swimming caddis pupa or damselfly nymph.

Another common variation features a body made from pheasant rump, the same feather used for the hackle. This is twisted around the hook shank, bound with tying silk, then trimmed to remove any stray hackle fibers. This dressing is usually called a "Self-Bodied Carey" or simply "Self Carey." A version called the "Six Pack" is tied the same way except the pheasant rump feather is dyed yellow, which usually results in converting the feather to an olive hue. Dyed feathers are used for both the body and hackle. The "Self-Bodied Carey" and "Six Pack" are often fished as damselfly nymph imitations.

Another version, the "Golden Carey," has a body of flat gold tinsel wound tightly around the hook shank and is used as an attractor pattern. Other variations have been tied with peacock herl or moose mane for the body. Most tyers have eliminated the tail, but some still add a short tail of golden pheasant tippet feathers.

Any of these versions, or all of them, are today among the patterns most likely to be found in the fly boxes of anglers throughout the Pacific Northwest and inland as far as Montana. The Carey Special is still used mostly as a stillwater fly, although some anglers have adopted it with good results for steelhead in rivers.

MY FIRST CAREY SPECIAL WAS GIVEN to me by my father. He loved to fish all his life, but a severe leg injury suffered as a young man made it impossible for him to wade rivers, so he took up the pursuit of Kamloops trout in the lakes of southern British Columbia. It was in those waters, not far from our home, that he introduced me to fly fishing in the days shortly after World War II.

He was not a fly tyer, so he had to purchase all the flies he used. This made him understandably reluctant to part with any that he felt had not yet delivered their full money's worth, which meant the flies he gave me usually had seen a good deal of hard service; some were nearly worn out. But to my six-year-old eyes, they were things of unblemished beauty.

That first Carey Special was in better shape than most of the flies he gave me. It had a thin body of brown wool and a full hackle of long, sweeping, reddish-brown pheasant rump. I never learned who tied it, but whoever it was deserves credit for making a nearly indestructible fly, one that not only survived several seasons of use by my father but several more in my youthful hands without suffering much visible wear. Its eventual fate was the best that could happen to any fly: I hooked a heavy fish that broke my gut leader and escaped with the Carey Special in its mouth. In all the years since, there have been few flies whose loss I felt more keenly.

5

UNTIL THAT FISH TOOK IT FROM ME SO RUDELY, my first Carey Special resided in a round plastic fly box. The box was divided into eight wedge-shaped compartments, like pieces of a pie. The lid rotated and had a little wedge-shaped door in it; the idea was to turn the lid until the door was positioned over the compartment containing the specific fly you wanted, then open the door, reach in and take out the fly. At first I had scarcely enough flies to keep one in each compartment, but that didn't stop me from continually rotating the lid and opening the door to inspect and admire the few I did have.

I thought that fly box was just about the niftiest gadget I'd ever seen. I used it many years, adding more flies as I went along until every compartment was nearly full. I'm not sure what finally happened to that box; it might still be around somewhere, possibly buried in my fishing closet, an angler's midden of discarded tackle, clothing and other gear. If some future archaeologist ever should excavate my closet, he'll be able to tell—no doubt to his great amusement—exactly what flies I was using and what fishing clothes I was wearing at any point in my life. He might even find that old round plastic fly box.

That box was the first of many I have owned. Its convenience and ease of use taught me early on that a good, well-designed container for flies is something to be valued. Few anglers think about this; their usual preoccupation is with rods, reels and lines. These, of course, are all essential fly-fishing tools, but the attention devoted to them should not be at the expense of other important items— including fly boxes.

A GOOD FLY BOX SHOULD BE MADE OF DURABLE, non-corrosive material. It should be easy to carry, small enough to fit in a vest pocket or tackle bag, easy to open, and convenient to use. It should provide storage for as many flies as possible, and provide it in an organized fashion so its owner can quickly find the specific pattern he wants. It also should be well suited for the particular type of fishing its owner wishes to do; for example, one probably would want a box made of noncorrosive materials for saltwater flies, while a metal box might do for freshwater trout patterns. The aesthetic value or appearance of a fly box also is important to most anglers and should be considered.

I have tried some fly boxes, found them wanting and subsequently discarded them; others proved so well suited to their purpose that I have carried them until they developed the patina of old age. A recent census revealed that I currently own twenty-eight fly boxes, representing many different shapes, sizes and methods of construction. Perhaps even more astounding than the number of boxes is the fact that nearly all of them are stuffed almost to capacity with flies.

Ten boxes hold trout flies. Others hold flies for steelhead, sea-run cutthroat, Pacific salmon, bonefish, and Atlantic salmon. One is reserved exclusively for flies acquired during my trips to New Zealand; I keep them separate so I can find them easily if I should ever be lucky enough to go there again. Another box holds some of the old British Columbia patterns inherited from my father, which I keep for both sentimental and historic reasons. Yet another small box, now empty, was once owned by my late friend and mentor Letcher Lambuth, noted bamboo-rod builder and the first man to study Northwest trout-stream insects. I have also kept it for sentimental and historic reasons.

Most of my fly boxes are made of plastic or a combination of plastic and foam. They are of simple construction and cost relatively little but do the job well. Most are unmarked, except for the labels I have put upon them, but several bear the inscribed logo of W.W. Doak & Sons, the famous fly shop on the banks of the Miramichi River. The boxes and most of the flies in them were purchased at Doak's.

A couple of boxes are notable for their ornamental value. One is a handsome, hand-made cedar fly box holding several steelhead flies; I received both box and flies in trade for a book. Another, also beautifully hand-made from wood, has several magnetic strips inside to hold flies in place. It was a gift from my friend Alec Jackson, well-known fly tyer and angling antiquarian. Although the box is certainly sturdy enough to take fishing, I consider it far too handsome to risk doing so; instead it occupies an honored place on my bookshelf.

The English-made Wheatley metal fly box is generally considered the ultimate in such appliances and I am fortunate to own a pair of these, both gifts. They are strong, durable and attractive, with highly polished surfaces that gleam with the essence of quality. Each has the capacity to hold a good number of flies in individual metal clips and I use them for my very best steelhead flies, mostly patterns given me by tyers more accomplished than I am.

Wheatley fly boxes are expensive and ownership of one is usually considered a matter of pride by anglers conscious of such things—sort of the piscatorial equivalent of taking your date to the prom in a Rolls Royce. If James Bond were a fly fisher, he would undoubtedly have a Wheatley fly box (probably with built-in hidden flame thrower and crypto machine).

Somewhat lower on the ladder of prestige, but nearly the equal of the Wheatley in serviceability, is the Perrine metal fly box. These come in a bewildering variety of sizes and configurations, and while they lack some of the aesthetic appeal of the Wheatley, they are still strong, durable and handsome. I have a matched pair, each a little smaller than a paperback book. Each has rows of individual clips inside, similar to the Wheatley, and I use them for steelhead flies I tie myself—one box for dry flies and low-water patterns, the other for wet flies. They are so similar in appearance that I can tell them apart only by the dent in the cover of the wet-fly box, a souvenir of having been dropped carelessly on a riverside rock.

Both the Wheatley and Perrine metal boxes have served me well. Their only disadvantage is that they won't make it through airport security checks; you must always take them out of your bag and open them for inspection.

Five small plastic boxes hold my assortment of sea-run cutthroat and Pacific salmon flies. Four of these are alike, each with six small compartments and a flip-up lid. I keep unused flies in these boxes. The fifth box opens like a book and has a foam lining on both sides; I use it for flies that already have been fished at least once in saltwater. These must be kept separate so there is no possibility they could spread corrosion to the hooks of unused flies in the other boxes. The foam-lined box is my saltwater equivalent of a lamb's-wool patch on a fishing vest.

Three other foam-lined plastic boxes—the ones with the W.W. Doak logo on their lids—hold my selection of Atlantic salmon flies. Most of these are flies I purchased from Doak's or tied myself for use on the Miramichi, but one box also holds patterns tied by my friend Bill Jollymore for use on Nova Scotia's beautiful Margaree.

Two other boxes hold bonefish flies. One is a small, transparent plastic box with a lift-up lid and six compartments. The other, also made of plastic, is much more elaborate; it has two trays inside, each with its own compartments, and when the lid is opened one tray lifts to expose the other. I have carried this box across the flats of Christmas Island in the Pacific and Turneffe Island in the Caribbean while searching for bonefish. Just how it came into my possession is something of a story; more about that later.

AS FOR MY TROUT FLIES, most are kept in nine small, translucent plastic fly boxes, each with six separate compartments. These fit neatly into slots in a rectangular box that serves as sort of a streamside "filing cabinet" (a tenth slot holds a stream thermometer). The rectangular box, originally made to hold 16-mm. movie film containers, was given me by a photographer about the time 16-mm. movie film was becoming obsolete. He also gave me many round metal film containers, which turned out to be the perfect size and shape to hold spools of leader material.

Each of the nine plastic boxes in the "filing cabinet" is labeled to indicate the type of flies it holds so I can easily find the box I want; after that it's a simple matter to open the lid and take out a specific pattern. The nine boxes, with their total of fifty-four compartments, provide storage for wet, dry, nymph and streamer patterns. Some compartments hold many duplicates of the same fly; others hold many different flies of the same basic type.

I keep very small flies—size 20 or smaller—in a separate foam-lined box. Such tiny patterns are too difficult to remove from the compartments in the plastic boxes that fit into the "filing cabinet."

I usually carry this "filing cabinet" and most of the rest of my fishing gear in a large tackle box. The box was intended for bait or lure fishermen—it came with compartments for a bait jar, lure and plug storage and so forth—but a little work with a hacksaw and sandpaper quickly converted it to suit my fly-fishing purposes. The alterations were all on the inside, however, so the box's outward appearance remains unchanged and occasionally it has been the target of derisive jibes from fly-fishing friends. I don't mind, though; it works for me.

The tackle box goes with me whenever I fish from a boat. When I plan to wade, I remove the boxes containing the flies I want and put them in the pockets of one of my fishing vests, then leave the "filing cabinet" and tackle box at home.

Anyone who spends very much time fly fishing eventually comes up with some sort of system for organizing and carrying flies. The "filing cabinet" is mine. It might not work for everyone, but there are plenty of other options to choose from. Nearly all fly-fishing catalogues feature large selections of fly boxes, ranging from translucent plastic cubes with built-in magnifiers to large, multi-trayed containers (not really very different from my "filing cabinet") attached to shoulder straps that allow an angler to carry them on his chest. The catalogues describe elaborate boxes featuring an "air-tight seal, recessed silicone gasket and positive locking system" or those made of "rugged glass-impregnated Delrin plastic with a clear polycarbonate top." For those with aesthetic considerations in mind, there are expensive hand-made wooden boxes or hand-tooled suede and leather fly wallets lined with sheep's fleece. Among metal fly boxes, the Wheatley remains the top of the line, and since foam is big these days even Wheatley is now making foam-lined boxes.

At the other end of the scale are the little translucent plastic fly boxes like those I use in my "filing cabinet." These don't last forever—I've had to replace some of them two or three times—but as of this writing they are still available for as little as $2.50 each, and they continue to work well for my purposes.

WHEN I BEGAN TYING FLIES, the Carey Special was one of the first patterns I tied. In those days the popular style still was to tie the pheasant rump hackle very full, and at first I had trouble making it behave in the fashion I wanted. The late Roy Patrick, who then owned Patrick's Fly Shop in Seattle, showed me how to bind the hackle down so the fibers pointed in the right direction, and after that I began tying Careys in many different sizes and colors. I used them just about everywhere I fished.

I discovered that a version with a black chenille body and a very sparse gray pheasant hackle tied on a size 10 or 12 hook made a passable imitation of a cased caddis larva. It proved deadly when I tried drifting it in the current of the North Fork of the Sultan River where it flows into Spada Lake, a reservoir in the Cascade foothills. Rainbow and cutthroat trout were always waiting around submerged stumps in the inlet, and they darted out and slammed the fly with uncommon violence. They weren't large—fourteen or fifteen inches was about tops—but they were fat and strong and great fun on a light fly rod.

I also found that a Carey Special with a body of hot orange chenille was very effective in lakes with thick algae blooms. Summer blooms are common in the fertile waters of British Columbia and the Columbia Basin, but the brightly colored body of the fly remained visible to trout even when the water was clouded with algae.

Washington State's now-famous Lenice Lake was in its first great flush of productivity when I began fishing it in the late 1960s.

Formed by irrigation seepage, the lake had risen in a desert coulee just east of the Columbia River, drowning thickets of sagebrush and greasewood. In October, when the water cooled, big rainbow trout would feed around submerged sagebrush roots in the shallows and I discovered they would hit a fluorescent green Carey Special with jackhammer force. Their average weight was about four pounds and some were larger. It was wonderful fishing, but there was nothing subtle about it; an eight-pound-test leader and a heavy hand were necessary to keep the fish from breaking off in the sagebrush.

The Carey Special has fetched many memorable trout for me. I remember one that came on a day which I noted in my diary must have been "one of the wettest in earth's history." I had driven to Price's Lake on the Olympic Peninsula, which at the time was served by a ramshackle fishing resort, a rundown little camp my friend Enos Bradner once called "the worst place in the State of Washington." It had been raining for days but the rain seemed to be falling even harder the day I went there; negotiating the dirt road to the camp was like swimming upstream to spawn. The old couple who ran the place said I was the first fisherman they had seen for a week; they really meant I was the first idiot they'd seen for a week, but they were too polite to say so. I paid them a modest sum for boat rental and walked down through the sopping jungle to the dock.

Only two boats were still afloat, and those just barely; the others all had filled with rainwater and sunk next to the dock. It took a long time to bail the water out of one of the two remaining boats, and once I got out on the lake the heavy rain required more bailing. But I managed to keep the boat afloat for five very long, very wet hours during which the fishing was just interesting enough to keep me from seeking a warm fire and dry clothes.

Using Carey Specials, I landed two rainbow, three cutthroat and three brook trout, none larger than twelve inches, and lost one much larger rainbow. Then, late in the afternoon, while I was fishing an orange-bodied Carey that gleamed like a flashlight in the rain-speckled water, I had a strong pull from an invisible fish. It fought deeply, which made me think it was a brook trout, and I could feel it shake its head, usually the sign of a heavy fish. When it finally came to the surface and displayed its flashy colors, the judgment of brook trout was confirmed.

I led the fish to my net and the fly pulled out just as the mesh closed around its writhing flanks. It was a seventeen-inch female brookie, thick and deep, and it pulled the scale down to the two and one-half-pound mark—not huge, but much larger than average in a part of the world where big brook trout are uncommon. It remains the largest brook trout I have ever caught in my native state.

THESE DAYS I MOST OFTEN FISH the Carey Special in Dry Falls Lake. The south arm of Dry Falls occupies a long, narrow fissure in the desert, pressing up against the face of a towering basalt cliff on its western shore. The water along the base of the cliff is surprisingly shallow, only two or three feet deep in most places, and in the fall large rainbow trout sometimes patrol the edge of the cliff seeking food. Their presence is usually revealed by a succession of quiet, subtle rises—or perhaps the word "rise" is meant to describe something more definitive than the tiny disturbances made by these fish, usually nothing more than little creases or wrinkles in the surface. These small disturbances are difficult to see, but once you do see them you will know a trout is there and feeding, most probably on small dragonfly nymphs.

These subtle rises mark the trout's progress along the face of the cliff and can be used to gauge the pace and rhythm of its feeding. The fishing technique is to cast to the place where you expect the next rise will occur, give the trout time enough to reach the spot, then twitch the fly once or twice. Most often the fish take the fly very softly and it almost requires a safecracker's fingers to detect the slight feeling of resistance on the line. But when you lift your rod, all hell breaks loose.

The Carey Special is by far the best fly for this fishing, still serving Colonel Carey's original purpose by imitating a dragonfly nymph. Aquatic plants around the shoreline of Dry Falls and other Columbia Basin lakes are full of these nymphs in the fall, when they represent the largest prey available to trout. The immature nymphs, probably due to hatch the following spring, are usually small enough to be matched by a fly tied on a No. 8 hook. They are nearly always some shade of green, ranging from dark olive to a sort of lime.

To imitate these nymphs I tie size 8 Carey Specials with bodies of chenille, Swannundaze, Body Glass, Larva Lace or V-Rib, all in slightly different shades of green. Usually it takes a little experimenting to determine which shade is the trouts' preference on any given day, but that's part of the fun. Sometimes a very small difference in color can make the difference between fishing success and failure.

My diary is filled with accounts of large rainbow and brown trout taken from Dry Falls in October on Carey Specials, including one rainbow that liked the fly so much it took it twice. The first time I hooked it, the fish ran into the heavy weed growth, broke my leader and escaped with the fly. I tied on another fly, resumed fishing, and about a half hour later had another strike. I landed a thick-sided rainbow that still had my original Carey Special stuck in its jaw, trailing about two feet of leader tippet.

But not all trout are as obliging—or as dumb—as that one.

OF THE FIFTY-FOUR COMPARTMENTS in the nine boxes that fit into my portable "filing cabinet" of flies, no fewer than seven are reserved for different versions of the Carey Special—more than for any other pattern. One whole box holds nothing but Careys. Three of its six compartments have patterns tied with bodies in various shades of green, ranging from dark olive to bright chartreuse. The other compartments hold Careys with red, orange and black bodies. A single compartment in another box is reserved for Self-Bodied Careys and Six-Packs.

The hook sizes of these flies range from 4 to 12, including a few of the long-shank variety. Some of the flies have been in use so long their colors have begun to fade, while others bear the unmistakable marks of sharp trout teeth. Then there are the bright new ones tied recently to replace others that wore out or were rudely stolen by trout stronger than my leader tippets.

All are different from the pattern Colonel Carey fashioned on the shore of Arthur Lake so many years ago, and if he were alive today he'd probably have trouble making the connection between them and his original fly. The only thing they have in common is the hackle, and my flies have little of that while his had a great deal.

But that little is enough to keep the Colonel's name attached to the pattern even after all the changes it has undergone. The Carey Special is the greatest and grandest of all Pacific Northwest trout fly patterns, one of the very few flies I have fished in all my nearly sixty years of angling experience. I suspect it will still be in use sixty years from now.

2

SKUNK

Hook: No. 4-12
Tying thread: Black
Tail: Saddle hackle fibers dyed red
Body: Black chenille
Rib: Silver tinsel
Wing: White polar bear hair, bucktail or calftail
Hackle: Saddle hackle fibers dyed black, tied down as beard

IN THE VERNACULAR OF ANGLERS, the word "skunk" usually means a day without fish. Happily, the fly pattern called the Skunk does not derive its name from that origin; instead, its name comes from the colors of the fly, which closely resemble those of a common woodland animal known for its highly odiferous venom.

To avoid confusion with a term that usually denotes lack of angling success, perhaps it would have been better if the fly had been named the Polecat instead of the Skunk. But Skunk it is, and by that name it has become one of the most widely known and trusted of all summer steelhead fly patterns.

The Skunk resembled its namesake even more in the past than it does now. Old pattern books give the dressing with an underwing of black bucktail, black bear hair or even black skunk fur topped by a wing of white bucktail or polar bear hair. The result was a black wing with a white stripe down the middle, very much like the backside of the animal for which the fly is named. Most modern tyers have dropped the black underwing, and since polar bear hair has become scarce and illegal to use, calftail, bucktail or artificial hair is now most often used as a substitute.

Except for those changes, the original dressing has remained pretty much intact through the years, with one important exception. The exception is called the Green-Butt Skunk, sometimes identified by even less tasteful names. As the sobriquet suggests, the pattern incorporates a butt section consisting of a few turns of fluorescent green chenille. This adds a spot of color to the traditional dark pattern and some anglers place great faith in this, although I have caught fish on both versions and have yet to see much difference between them.

Just who tied the first Skunk is a subject of continuing debate.

Trey Combs, in his milestone book *Steelhead Fly Fishing,* quotes Frank Moore of Steamboat Inn on Oregon's North Umpqua River as saying the pattern was first tied by Mildred Krogel of Roseburg, Oregon, for use by her husband, Lawrence, on the North Umpqua. But Combs also says the pattern was developed independently by the late Wes Drain of Seattle, who once held the Washington State record for largest steelhead on a fly. Other sources also credit Drain.

I fished several times with Wes but never thought to ask him about the Skunk; he was such a modest, self-effacing man that if he did have anything to do with the pattern it probably would have been difficult to get him to admit it. Considering the number of different ingredients in the pattern, however, it is unlikely two fly tyers working independently could have arrived at the same dressing. Since the Skunk seems to have achieved popularity in Oregon before it was widely used elsewhere, I suspect the Krogel story is the more credible of the two. But the jury is still out, and probably always will be.

YEARS AGO, IN ANOTHER BOOK, I wrote that the Skykomish Sunrise was my favorite steelhead fly. It was true at the time—but that was then and this is now. And now, when I fish a wet fly for steelhead, the Skunk is usually my first choice.

Why the change? It's not because I have lost any affection or respect for the Skykomish Sunrise. It's a fly that remains as beautiful as its name, a bright pattern that shines like a Christmas-tree ornament in the dark waters of a winter river. But it's precisely because the Skykomish Sunrise is a traditional winter steelhead pattern that it is no longer my first choice, because these days I rarely fish for winter steelhead. Winter rivers have become too crowded with anglers and not crowded enough with fish, and their cold water has begun to do unpleasant things to my aging joints. Now I fish mostly for summer steelhead, and for that purpose the Skunk is as dependable a wet-fly pattern as any I know. Its peculiar combination of black, red, white and silver has deadly appeal for steelhead.

In making the transition from winter to summer steelhead fly fishing, I began to establish an annual routine. I would start each summer on the North Fork of the Stillaguamish, where the steelhead run usually peaks by mid-July. When the best of the North Fork run was over, I would begin searching for fish in the little Green River near Mount St. Helens, and when that run was past its late-summer prime, the fall steelhead run in the Wenatchee River would draw me like a magnet. Sometimes I would interrupt this routine and journey to other rivers—the Sol Duc, Bogachiel, Elwha or Duckabush on the Olympic Peninsula, the Kalama or the Sauk, Oregon's mighty Deschutes, or the Coquihalla in British Columbia. But none of these captured my affection as much as the Stillaguamish, the Green or the Wenatchee.

The Skunk was a good fly in all of them, and not just for steelhead. Once in the Green River I hooked a strong fish I first thought was a steelhead, but when it finally surrendered after a long, spirited fight I was surprised to discover it was a whitefish, the largest I have ever seen. I learned later it probably would have qualified as a record, but I wouldn't have kept the fish even if I'd known because I don't believe in fishing records. The Skunk also brought me some large Dolly Varden and large sea-run cutthroat.

I went through Skunk patterns at a prodigious rate. On one two-day trip to the Deschutes I started with a dozen Skunks in my fly box and came home with only two—and each of those had bent hooks and other signs of wear. Most of the others had been torn apart by angry steelhead, broken off by others that simply refused to be landed, or lost on river-bottom snags.

That trip was harder on my fly selection than most, but no matter where I fished it seemed I was always running short of Skunks. In tying replacements I tried to follow the traditional dressing, but sometimes I would run out of some of the materials needed for the pattern. Naturally this always happened at a time or place where it was inconvenient or impossible to get more, so I would try to make do with the materials I had. Sometimes what I had seemed to work better than the materials in the original dressing.

Once, when I ran out of red-dyed saddle hackle fibers for the tail, I substituted dyed red swan instead. It proved too stiff and lifeless in the water, so in desperation I next tried frayed-out strands of red rayon floss, and this worked better—so much better, in fact, that I decided to keep on using it. Another time, when I discovered I was out of silver tinsel, I used gold mylar ribbing instead, and liked the look of it so much I decided that it, too, would become a permanent part of my own personal version of the Skunk.

I had never been quite satisfied with polar bear hair or bucktail for the wing. I managed to acquire a large stock of polar bear hair when it was still legal and plentiful, so lack of supply wasn't a problem; I just thought polar bear hair was a little too stiff for lifelike movement in the water. I liked bucktail even less; it was brittle, broke easily and was even stiffer than polar bear hair. Artificial hair had yet to come on the market, so it wasn't an option. I tried calftail and ended up tying many Skunks with white calftail wings; they worked well enough to make me think the problem was solved, although I continued to keep a lookout for something better.

Then I discovered white rabbit fur. I had bought some to use in another pattern—I don't now even remember what it was—when it occurred to me that rabbit fur might make the ultimate Skunk wing. Its fine, soft fibers were of the purest white and seemed to come alive in the water, giving an illusion of movement that even calftail couldn't match. Rabbit fur also was easier to shape and position on the hook than anything else I'd tried. That was important because I'm not a fast tyer and I had been looking for ways to save tying time while preserving the look of the original Skunk pattern. Using white rabbit for the wing appeared one way to do this.

Eliminating the black hackle beard was another time-saving tactic I thought would not compromise the effectiveness of the pattern, and so it proved to be. Both steps saved time, enabling me to tie more Skunks, and the resulting bastard version caught fish as well as the original pattern ever did.

So that is how I tie the Skunk now: Frayed red floss tail, black chenille body, gold rib, white rabbit wing—and that's all. It's definitely a shorthand version of the original, but it still does the job nicely and I can turn out flies faster than I ever could following the original pattern.

I still do carry a selection of the originals, however. Some years ago my friend Alec Jackson gave me a series of traditional Skunks tied on low-water Atlantic salmon hooks, some as small as size 12. I fish them on a floating line, which means I've managed to avoid losing any of them on snags, and they have seen so much hard use their once-bright tinsel has become tarnished and the luster of their polar bear hair wings has all but disappeared. But they are still recognizable as Skunks faithful to the original pattern, and I can and do fall back on them if my bastard version ever fails to work. To me it is the best of both worlds.

AT THE TIME I STARTED FISHING the North Fork of the Stillaguamish, it had a fly-fishing-only season that expired October 31. Beginning the next day, anglers could fish the river with bait, lures or almost anything else, and many did.

This did not sit well with the fly anglers who fished the river regularly; the hordes of bait and lure fishermen who descended on the river November 1 crowded fly fishers off the stream and killed many of the steelhead they had released earlier, defeating the purpose of the catch-and-release ethic many fly fishers were then beginning to embrace.

So fly fishers began lobbying state management authorities to extend the fly-only season another month, until the end of November. At first these efforts were firmly resisted—it's always easier for fisheries managers to do nothing than to do something—but in the face of steadily mounting pressure, the State Game Commission finally agreed to extend the fly-fishing-only season to the end of November on a trial basis for one year. If catch statistics showed that enough fly fishers used the river during November of the trial season, then the extension would be made permanent; if not, the October 31 closure would be reinstated.

The message to fly fishers was clear: Use it or lose it.

At the time this happened, in the early 1970s, the state's primary method of monitoring the steelhead sport catch was through punch cards issued to anglers. When a steelhead was caught, the angler was required to punch his card immediately and make note of the date and the name of the river. At the end of the season, the punch cards were supposed to be mailed back to the state or turned in to authorized tackle shops, where they would be collected and forwarded. Fisheries managers would then use the cards to total the catch for each river; those numbers, in turn, would help determine future minimum spawning escapements and bag limits.

The returned punch cards also could be used to gauge angler effort, and that was how the state intended to judge the November trial fly-fishing season on the North Fork. If many punch cards were returned showing November catches in the North Fork, that would be evidence fly fishers were taking advantage of the extended season; if not, that would be evidence they weren't.

Among the anglers who had lobbied hard to extend the fly-fishing season through November was a young man who worked as a clerk at a Seattle-area fly shop. We'll call him Don, although that's not his real name; his real name has been changed to protect the guilty—for Don, as you will see, was certainly guilty of something. The exact nature of his "crime" has never been determined, although it might have been forgery. Whatever it was, it was committed for a good cause.

This is what Don did: When the steelhead season ended and anglers started bringing their punch cards into the fly shop to deposit them in a box left there for the purpose, Don waited until they were gone, retrieved their cards from the box, added a few more punches to each card and indicated that the fictional fish had been caught in the North Fork of the Stillaguamish during November.

Nobody knows how many cards he punched, or how many punches he added to each of them, but when all the cards had been returned to the state and biologists totaled up the year's catch, the results showed more steelhead had been caught in the North Fork of the Stillaguamish during November than any other river in the state. Based on this "overwhelming" response to the November trial fly-fishing-only season, the State Game Commission voted to extend the season through November permanently.

The fly-fishing-only season on the North Fork remains open until November 30 to this day. Who says crime doesn't pay?

THE EXTENDED FLY-FISHING-ONLY SEASON was one of many reasons I didn't hesitate when I was offered a chance to acquire a fishing cabin on the North Fork. The cabin was on a small lot owned by two old friends, Enos Bradner and Sandy Bacon, just downstream from the little community of Oso, where Deer Creek joins the North Fork.

Deer Creek is the North Fork's most significant tributary and once hosted a great natural run of wild summer steelhead. Thanks mostly to savage logging practices, the run had declined seriously by the mid-1970s, but the few fish that still returned to Deer Creek often held in the stretch of river below Oso, fronted by Bradner's and Bacon's cabin. Bradner had grown too old to wade the river or look after the cabin and Bacon had moved to Portland, so they decided jointly to sell the place. When Brad asked if I knew anyone who might want to buy it, I quickly made an offer.

In doing so I was also making a commitment to the North Fork, probably at the expense of the other rivers I had come to know and love. In a way it was like entering into marriage; although I didn't have to promise to forsake all other rivers, I knew in effect that was what I was doing—pledging my fishing troth to the North Fork. At first that made me as nervous as a groom, but I soon found that being committed to a single river, and getting to know it intimately, was far more satisfying than having a casual acquaintance with many rivers. Since then, through both sickness and health, the North Fork has remained the chief object of my summer fly-fishing affections.

I was still pretty much exclusively a wet-fly fisherman when I began fishing the North Fork regularly, and the Skunk was the fly I used most often. Early in the season, when the water was high, I would fish it on a sinking line; later, when the river dropped, I would switch to a sink-tip line. By late August, when the North Fork was low enough to show its bones, I would sometimes use a floating line.

But the Skunk was not the only fly I used. There were at least three other patterns I used regularly, not because the Skunk lacked effectiveness but because the others were especially well suited to certain conditions. These were the Oso Special, the Omnibus and the Fall Favorite.

THE OSO SPECIAL WAS NAMED FOR THE COMMUNITY where Deer Creek enters the North Fork. The pattern's origin is unknown to me, but its absence from older pattern books suggests it was developed fairly recently. It was first shown to me by Rod Belcher, a long-time Seattle radio sports announcer.

There's nothing subtle or aesthetically pleasing about the Oso Special; in fact, it's a fairly brutal, in-your-face kind of fly pattern. It's also a bulky fly, tied on a heavy hook with materials that absorb water easily, so it sinks quickly. The pattern is simple: a short tail of fluorescent hot-orange floss, body of thick fluorescent hot-orange chenille over the rear three-quarters and black chenille over the front quarter, and a wing of black bear hair extending the length of the body. Some tyers also add a black hackle, but most versions I've seen have no hackle.

The Oso Special's color combination is readily visible even in murky water and that, combined with its fast-sinking qualities, makes it a good early season pattern when the river is running high and fast and dirty. I've caught fish on the Oso Special in water conditions so poor I had to question my sanity for fishing at all.

For these reasons, the Oso Special is often the very first fly I use at the beginning of the season. Sometimes I fish it on a high-density line that takes it down to the river bottom where it flirts dangerously with rocks. It's not the way I like to fish, but sometimes it's a matter of either fishing that way or not at all.

Bumping a fly along the bottom also results in many hang-ups, broken leaders and lost flies, but I don't mind losing Oso Specials because they are quick and easy to tie and there's nothing very attractive about them. To tell the truth, I don't much like the Oso Special, but for fishing under marginal water conditions there's hardly anything better.

THE OMNIBUS WAS CREATED in the 1950s by Len Hunton, a charter member of the Washington Fly Fishing Club. It was developed for sea-run cutthroat in the rivers flowing into Willapa Bay, a huge estuary on the Washington coast. Examining the stomach contents of cutthroat he caught, Hunton found they often had been feeding on crayfish whose chief colors were green, yellow and red, so he set out to create a fly incorporating those colors. The result looked nothing like a crayfish, but it nevertheless proved deadly for sea-runs; it worked equally well when Hunton tried it for steelhead.

In an article he once wrote about the fly, Hunton said he tied it on many different types and sizes of hooks, "from No. 6 Irish Limerick streamer hooks to No. 1 to No. 6 2X strong or 3X fine, depending upon whether the trip is for cutts or steelhead. Prior to the availability of sinking lines, the hook on occasion was wrapped with .020 lead wire for heavy steelhead waters."

Like Hunton, I began fishing the Omnibus for sea-run cutthroat and only later tried it as a steelhead pattern. It quickly evolved into my "last-resort" fly—the pattern most likely to move a steelhead when all others fail. Obviously this applies only when you know a fish is there, and because fish are very difficult to see in the North Fork of the Stillaguamish, just about the only way to tell one is there is to see it roll, jump, or come to a fly without taking. When any of those things happens, the technique is to keep changing flies and continue to cover the fish until it takes or you give up. For me, the fly that usually takes the fish, if it can be taken at all, is the Omnibus.

So why not fish one all the time? I suppose it's because I have so much confidence in the Skunk that I continue to use it as my main searching fly whenever water conditions permit. A steelhead that is ready to take will usually grab a Skunk the first time it swings past its nose; maybe the same would be true for an Omnibus, but I prefer to keep it in reserve for difficult fish. One reason is that the Omnibus is more difficult and time-consuming to tie than the Skunk, so I never have as many in my fly box and I hate to lose one. Maybe that's the real reason I continue to use the Skunk as my main exploratory pattern.

Yet there have been occasions when I fished the Omnibus successfully as an exploratory fly. One summer brought more than the usual amount of rain and the North Fork was still running high in late August. I had spent the day at my cabin dodging rain showers and when I finally went out on the river early in the evening, the air had been washed clean and held a hint of chill. The sun was low in the western sky, shining with the color of a ripening squash. Little stone-flies and cream-colored mayflies were lifting off the river and dancing in the long rays of the setting sun, and streamers of silk from broken spider webs floated past on a gentle breeze. It was a wonderful evening.

Without thinking much about it, I put on a high-density line and a Skunk and started fishing well up in the Elbow Hole. I had fished more than halfway down when I saw a fish porpoise, probably a salmon, and when it failed to respond to a Skunk I switched to an Omnibus on the off chance that the fish was a steelhead. This time the Omnibus didn't work either, so I fished on down to the end of the run, waded out and walked the short distance downstream to a little slick at the head of what we then called the Rip-Rap Pool.

Too lazy to change flies, I resumed fishing with the Omnibus and had covered about half the length of the slick when a fish took with a hard strike and ran immediately. Heading for shore, I missed see-ing the fish jump, although I heard its splash. Once ashore I man-aged to recover some line, but then the fish ran again and jumped a second time. Suddenly the line went slack and I felt certain I had lost the fish, but when I started reeling in, the line came tight and once more I felt a throbbing weight at the other end.

The fish ran several more times, never far but always strongly, and when I finally brought it close enough for a good look I was surprised to see how small it was: a hatchery fish (with clipped adi-pose fin) of only about three pounds. It had given an extraordinar-ily good account of itself, one worthy of a fish twice its size, and when I finally eased it up onto the sandy bank, the Omnibus was lodged firmly in the corner of its jaw.

The next day I drove to the Sauk River. Still flushed with the success of the Omnibus, I tied on another. I had fished only a short while when I hooked and landed an eight-pound chinook salmon, a male with a big kype on its lower jaw and a pleasing strawberry hue on its flanks. Once again the Omnibus had succeeded as an exploratory fly.

The pattern, as originally conceived by Len Hunton, includes a medium silver tinsel tip, a tail of red and yellow marabou (with red on top), a full body of peacock herl, four turns of medium silver tinsel ribbing, three turns each of red and yellow dyed saddle hackle, and a wing of white bucktail, polar bear hair or calftail. The white wing, red and yellow hackle and tail, and peacock herl body give this fly an unusual combination of light and dark colors, which I believe is one reason for its success.

With the usual arrogance of fly tyers, I have made my own alterations to this pattern. I now tie it on a No. 4 gold-plated hook, mostly just for show, and use flat gold tinsel for the ribbing instead of silver. As with the Skunk, I use white rabbit for the wing, again because I believe it gives more lifelike movement in the water. Len Hunton once viewed these changes and approved of them. Whether they have improved the effectiveness of his original pattern is questionable, but my slightly altered version has many times proven itself on hard-to-please steelhead. It doesn't always work, of course—what fly does?—but it has done so often enough to win my confidence.

I LOVE THE FALL FAVORITE FOR ITS COLORS, its slim silhouette and its wonderfully alliterative name. As the name seems to demand, I fish this fly during fall months when the red and gold colors of streamside leaves match the colors of the fly. Under such circumstances it seems heresy to use any other pattern.

Trey Combs, in one of his earlier books, *Steelhead Fishing and Flies*, attributes the Fall Favorite to Lloyd Silvius of Eureka, California. Combs says Silvius created the pattern in 1946 to fish for fall-run steelhead in the Eel River. But Roy Patrick, in *Pacific Northwest Fly Patterns* (1970 edition), says just as authoritatively that the Fall Favorite was first tied by Butch Wilson of Arcata, California, and took a steelhead on British Columbia's Kispiox River that won an award from *Field & Stream* magazine. Who's right? Take your choice.

Although they attributed the fly to different tyers, Combs and Patrick did agree on the dressing: Body of flat silver tinsel, dyed red saddle hackle, hot orange bucktail, polar bear hair or calftail wing. Other pattern books, however, specify gold tinsel for the body and a hackle tied down as a beard, and that is the way I have always tied the Fall Favorite. I also like to use a No. 4 or 6 low-water Atlantic salmon hook and tie the pattern sparsely, then fish it on a floating line during fall low water.

That combination has resulted in some memorable catches. One late September morning I went out on the North Fork under a slate-gray sky and found the river running the color of weak tea after a recent rain. An old fungus-streaked salmon fled from my presence as I waded across the river, and I could see bright patches of gravel where spawning chum salmon had made their redds. Faded-yellow maple leaves drifted in the current and collected on upstream rock faces, while small corkscrews of sand and silt danced on the rocks' downstream sides, ephemeral little tornadoes of the river.

I fished each of the familiar places I had fished all summer long, but they neither looked nor felt as they had in August or July, nor did they fish the same; fall had changed the whole character of the river. Someone once said that you never cast twice into the same river, and the North Fork, changing every moment, proved the truth of that assertion.

It began to rain—a fine, gentle rain at first, growing steadily harder until at last I could scarcely see my fly in the spray of drops striking the water. Not that it mattered; I had seen nothing in the first two pools I fished, and nothing had come to my fly. I don't remember now what fly I started with, but in obeisance to the change of seasons I decided it was time for a Fall Favorite. I took one from my fly box, tied it on the end of my leader, and went on to the next pool.

I had made no more than a dozen casts when I was taken strongly by a good fish that ran all the way into the backing, jumping twice as it went. It had been a long time since the backing had been off the reel and some of the windings stuck together, so I picked at them frantically to free them up and give the fish more line. Finally the run came to an end and I recovered some line, but then the fish started again and took a second trip deep into the backing. Once more it stopped to rest and I got most of the line back before it started moving again, not swiftly this time but steadily and inexorably, heading downstream toward the tail of the pool. I followed, trying and failing to turn the fish, then watched in alarm as it went over the lip of the pool's tail-out and down into the fast water below.

The fish picked up speed in the fast water and again peeled all the line and much of the backing off the reel while I splashed after it. Finally the steelhead halted in a patch of quiet water inside a bend, giving me a chance to catch up, but when I did I discovered the line was wrapped around a rock and there was no sign of the fish. Thinking I'd lost it, I waded out to free the line; when it came free from the rock I again felt the fish's life and weight on the other end—but then saw I'd somehow managed to wrap four turns of fly line around my rod tip, which was in imminent danger of being broken if the fish should run again.

By then, however, the fish was too tired to do much of anything; it stayed quiet while I fumbled frantically until the line was free again. After that it was a fairly simple matter to lead the fish to the beach, where it revealed itself as a handsome buck, a hatchery fish with a pale rose stripe along its side. I judged its weight about six pounds and noted with satisfaction the Fall Favorite gleaming like a headlight in its upper jaw.

It was also a Fall Favorite that took one of the grandest fish I've ever caught, a fish I will always remember. It was near the end of a year when I had fished hard all summer, but the North Fork had been even more stingy than usual and I had little to show for my efforts. I had kept at it, however, and on this particular day I was fishing a Fall Favorite to match the colors of the advancing season.

Just above the slick at the head of the Rip-Rap Pool I hooked an enormous fish, a fish so strong that at first I could do nothing with it. It ran repeatedly back and forth through the pool, taking line far into the backing no fewer than seven times. Three times it leaped high out of the water, and from its bronze color and the way it was fighting I suspected it was a big king (chinook) salmon rather than a steelhead.

So it proved to be. After a long, wearying, thirty-five-minute fight, I finally eased it up on the beach—a great, bronze fish that measured forty inches long. I estimated its weight at twenty-five pounds.

I removed the Fall Favorite from its angular jaw and spent a long time resuscitating the fish; eventually its strength returned and it swam slowly away and disappeared in the amber water. It had taken the fly in the surface film on a floating line—highly unusual for a chinook salmon—but even more amazing was that I had fought the fish all that time, through all those runs and jumps, and landed it on a leader tippet that tested only six pounds in breaking strength.

That fish made my whole season.

IN RECENT YEARS I HAVE BEGUN USING the dry fly more often for summer steelhead, whenever water conditions in the fickle North Fork will permit. But when the river is high or the least bit dirty and a wet fly is essential, the Skunk remains my first choice while the Oso Special, Omnibus and Fall Favorite are always ready to perform their specific back-up roles.

As every angler should, I continue to question my choice of fly and my tactics for fishing it, but after more than a quarter of a century patrolling the pools and riffles of the North Fork, I think I have developed a good feel for what works and what doesn't, and these four patterns have won my confidence through repeated use and results.

Of them all, the Skunk is the one I have used longest. It is still the most reliable steelhead wet fly pattern I know. Often it's both the first and last fly I use in a day's fishing, and if it should fail to bring a fish, I will choose to believe it is the fault of the river and not the fault of the fly—for if a fish was there it surely would have taken a well-presented Skunk.

3

TDC

(THOMPSON'S DELECTABLE CHIRONOMID)

Hook: No. 8-16
Thread: Black
Body: Black wool or floss
Rib: Thin flat silver tinsel over body only (not thorax)
Thorax: Black wool or floss, thicker than body
Hackle: White ostrich herl

THE DEVELOPMENT OF A NEW FLY PATTERN is often a painstaking process that extends over several seasons. Many different combinations of colors or materials must be tried and fine-tuned until the tyer and the trout are both satisfied with the result; only then is the new pattern considered established and ready for use. Very rarely does a fly tyer get everything right on the first try.

But Richard B. (Dick) Thompson was one who did.

"I believe it was early spring of 1961, or perhaps '62, that Boyd Aigner and I were fishing one weekend in the Columbia Basin," Thompson now recalls. "We had heard about the fishing in Sand Lake [south of Ephrata, Washington] and decided it was worthy of investigation. We were in my 1959 American Motors Rambler, properly equipped with food, stove, sleeping bags and air mattresses. Also with fly-tying gear for replacements and, perhaps, new patterns.

"On Saturday we had the lake to ourselves, fishing from our small prams. . . . In the late afternoon surface activity by trout in the ten- to twelve-inch size range began and increased until most of the visible part of the lake was covered with rises. We could see nothing coming out of the water, however. Frustrating. No hits, no follows, no interest by any fish in our offerings of Carey Specials, Needlefly Nymphs, etc.

"I tied on a rather dark pattern, name, if any, unknown, and hooked and landed one of the ten-inchers. I looked at its stomach contents and found lots of black, white-striped pupae with little white collars near the head. Even though the rise was continuing, I decided to try to imitate these little things.

"The steering wheel of the Rambler was where the vise was fastened and it didn't take long to tie a few: a No. 10 wet-fly hook, black wool body, silver tinsel ribbing, enlarged thorax of black wool, a few turns of white ostrich herl around the head, and that was it.

"Back on the lake, I began casting to risers and was hooking fish on two casts out of three! I thought, hmmm, maybe something important here. Boyd had seen me go to the car and return to the lake a few minutes later, but didn't think anything of it until after I had taken five or six fish. [Then] he came over to see what it was all about. He, too, had made the odd hook-up, but not enough compared to the number of rising fish.

"Reluctantly, I gave him one of the patterns I had tied. And, of course, he too began hooking trout on a high ratio of casts.

"Thus an afternoon of exemplary fishing. The next thing we discussed was a name for this funny-looking imitation of a pupa of a . . . what? After I had done some research on limnological critters and ascertained that they were of the chironomid family, Boyd suggested that acronyms were popular at the time and gave it the title of TDC.

"What those letters meant was kept secret for quite a few years, but finally someone who did know helped spread the word that they stood for 'Thompson's Delectable Chironomid!'"

Delectable it was. The TDC was a nearly perfect imitation of the pupal stage of a chironomid; not only that, it was quick and easy to tie and proved highly durable in use. And it opened up a whole new frontier for fly fishers.

IN RETROSPECT, IT SEEMS PUZZLING THAT it took anglers so long to recognize the importance of the chironomid. A member of the order *Diptera* (true flies, or midges), the chironomid is found in stillwaters nearly everywhere, but is especially common in the high-desert lakes of the Cascade rainshadow, which extends all the way from northern California into British Columbia. Most of these waters are rich in aquatic life and blessed with long growing seasons, but the chironomid is arguably their most important single food source and virtually the only one available to trout from the very beginning of the season to the very end.

More than twenty-five hundred chironomid species have been identified. They come in many different colors and sizes, the largest nearly an inch long and the smallest scarcely larger than a pinpoint. They are most abundant in the shallows of fertile, eutrophic lakes with silty bottoms, a description that fits many waters in the Cascade rainshadow.

The chironomid larva is long, thin, segmented and cylindrical in shape and worm-like in appearance. Many species construct thin tubes of mud attached to the lake bottom; the larvae live inside these tubes and respirate by means of undulating movements. They feed on algae or plankton drifting in the water column. When metamorphosis is complete, the pupae emerge from the tube and hide briefly in bottom detritus until they are ready to hatch. Then each pupa begins a long, slow ascent to the surface, swimming upward with a rapid flexing motion of its body, much like a dog wagging its tail. When it reaches the surface, the pupa first hangs perpendicularly in the surface film, then gradually assumes a horizontal position while waiting for its wingcase to split and the adult winged insect to emerge.

Chironomids are most vulnerable to trout during this long, slow ascent to the surface and the period when they are hanging from or in the surface film waiting to hatch, and vast numbers find their way into trout stomachs. Freshly hatched adults also are sometimes taken while sitting on the surface waiting for their wings to dry. Later, after mating, adult female flies return to the water and skate across the surface to lay their eggs, and their tempting movements also bring many trout to the surface to feed.

Chironomids are the first insects to appear in the spring, often emerging through holes in the ice of higher-elevation lakes while most of the surface remains frozen. Their hatches peak in May or early June, depending on the latitude and elevation of the lake, but go on sporadically all through the summer and fall until the lake again freezes over. Thus the chironomid is a staple of the trout's diet through the entire season.

A heavy chironomid hatch is a sight to behold. Flies of several different sizes (and species) often hatch simultaneously, and the result is a veritable blizzard of insects hovering like smoke over the surface of a lake. The sound of their countless tiny wings beating at high speed creates a deep electric hum audible at considerable distances. A hatch of such proportions can be very uncomfortable for anglers who must contend with multitudes of insects bent on crawling into their eyes, nose, ears or mouth. This in itself is enough to drive a fisherman to distraction, but there is the added problem that his imitation is quite literally lost among an apparently infinite number of real insects on the water, so there is little chance of catching fish. At such times an angler is well advised to go ashore and spend the time tying flies while waiting for the hatch to subside. The fishing is certainly more comfortable, and usually much better, when emerging chironomids are less abundant.

Heavy or sparse, chironomid hatches are always highly visible, with insects rising from the surface amid the excited rises of pursuing trout. The aftermath of a hatch is also visible; the lake's surface is littered with hundreds of floating empty black-and-white pupal cases. The high visibility of the chironomid makes it all the more difficult to understand why fly fishers failed to develop imitations much earlier than they did.

One who did try was Bill Nation, the famous British Columbia fly tyer and guide. Nation was far ahead of his time in almost everything he did, including his efforts to imitate the chironomid. Sometime during the late 1920s or early 1930s he devised a fly intended to imitate the pupae of chironomids he observed hatching in British Columbia's Kamloops trout lakes. The pattern, called Nation's Black, was tied on a No. 8 hook and had a thin body of black floss, no rib, and a sparse "wing" of dark brown bucktail. That was all.

As an imitation, the Nation's Black left much to be desired. It wasn't very effective and never became popular with other anglers, and one is left with the impression that Nation was far more interested in trying to imitate some of the more spectacular forms of aquatic life inhabiting the Kamloops trout lakes, such as caddisflies, dragonflies and damselflies. His colorful, highly fanciful representations of these and other insects worked extremely well, although by modern definition we would not think of them as being very "imitative." Nevertheless, they became favorites of a whole generation of anglers while Nation's Black was all but forgotten.

Perhaps other anglers experimented with chironomid imitations; if so, their patterns have not survived. From the time of Nation's Black until the advent of the TDC in the early 1960s, the historical record is blank.

NOW RETIRED AFTER A CAREER as a federal fisheries biologist, Dick Thompson is a member of the Washington Fly Fishing Club in

Seattle. He introduced his TDC pattern to other members soon after its invention and they fished it with such success that its popularity spread rapidly. Before long it began appearing in fly-pattern books and soon was in widespread use in waters both east and west of the Cascades.

As usually happens with successful new patterns, other tyers were quick to launch variations. Many of these incorporated different colors—patterns with red, green or brown bodies soon appeared, designed to imitate pupae of those colors—but some tyers also tried different materials for the body (such as floss) or ribbing (white dental floss was a popular choice). The authors of these patterns also usually gave them different names, but they resembled the TDC so closely it was obvious they had been inspired by Thompson's pattern.

My first experience fishing the TDC was on Tunkwa Lake, British Columbia, noted for the intensity of its spring chironomid hatches. The day was windy and cold but the weather seemed to have no effect on the hatch, which was truly of monumental proportions. Chironomids of all sizes were emerging in countless numbers and each fresh gust of wind blew a cloud of them into my face. Adult flies crept inside my collar, sleeves and pants; so many gathered on the lenses of my sunglasses that I couldn't see, and it was an ongoing battle to keep them from trying to crawl inside my eyes, ears, nose and mouth.

The trout, meanwhile, were going crazy. Big fish—some five or six pounds or more—cruised around frantically, dorsals slicing through the surface as if they were sharks, open mouths swallowing dozens of hatching insects at a time. The lonely TDC at the end of my leader was utterly lost among the countless naturals, and I knew it. But I had come a long way to fish, so I wasn't about to give up. I covered rises for several hours without result; then, without warning, a heavy fish suddenly took my fly, ran quickly all the way to the backing, and disappeared as quickly as it had come. That was the only strike I had during a long, cold, bug-infested day.

It was the following April before I actually caught my first fish on a TDC. It was quite an ordinary fish—a ten-inch rainbow—and there was no way of knowing it would be the first of a great many I would take on this deadly pattern. In years to come my TDCs would account for hundreds of rainbow, cutthroat, brook trout, brown trout, whitefish and even a few landlocked Atlantic salmon. The TDC worked well wherever I fished it—in alpine lakes of the North Cascades, rainforest beaver ponds, high-desert lakes, even the slow-moving waters of a river slough.

But the place where I fished it most often, and with the greatest success, was Dry Falls Lake. The broad shallows of Dry Falls have been likened to a chalk stream without a current, and the comparison is apt. The shallows are carpeted with heavy weed growth, especially in the spring; the water is very clear and the trout are exceptionally shy and fussy. It's hard to catch fish consistently in these shallows, and that makes them among my favorite places to fish.

Most areas of the shallows are three to four feet deep during spring high water, although there are—or at least used to be—numerous deep cavities in the weed growth. Anglers called these places "black holes" and they were always worth fishing because trout would shelter in them. When chironomids were hatching, a TDC fished on a sinking line in these "black holes" was almost irresistible to trout. The same pattern fished on a floating line over the shallow weedy areas surrounding the "black holes" was similarly effective.

The first time I used a TDC at Dry Falls I landed fourteen trout. That seemed like a lot at the time, but it was often eclipsed in days to come; twenty- or thirty-fish days became the rule rather than the exception. Partly this was due to the liberal stocking policies and bag limits in effect at the time; Dry Falls wasn't exactly a put-and-take fishery, but it wasn't far from it. Most of the fish I caught there were rainbows in the twelve- to fourteen-inch class, with an occasional bruiser up to three pounds—one of few survivors of more than a single season in the lake (Dry Falls has no inlet stream where trout can spawn, so it is stocked annually). The lake also held small numbers of brown trout in the same size range, and it was always a treat to catch one or more of those.

THAT WAS THE KIND OF FISHING I ENJOYED AT Dry Falls for more than a decade before things began to change. For years fly fishers had lobbied the state to change regulations and stocking policies at the lake; eventually the state agreed to impose stricter angling rules, tighten bag limits, and reduce the number of trout stocked every year. These actions immediately resulted in an exponential increase in fishing pressure—something that always seems to happen when any type of "quality" regulation is imposed—along with a decrease in numbers of trout caught and an increase in their average size.

None of that was surprising. It was, in fact, just what the fly-fishing community wanted. But over the next few years something else happened that was surprising, at least to me: The TDC began to lose its effectiveness in Dry Falls. It still caught fish, but not with the same regularity as before.

One obvious reason was that the new stocking policy meant fewer trout were present to be caught, but that in itself didn't seem to account fully for the declining effectiveness of one of my favorite flies. Something else was going on and it took a while for me to understand what it was. At length I realized the combination of smaller bag limits, reduced numbers of fish and greatly increased angling pressure meant that a higher percentage of the trout in Dry Falls were being caught and released than ever before, and many were being caught on the TDC. Trout are not mental giants, but even the dumbest can learn to recognize a threat if it's repeated often enough—and after being caught two or three times on a TDC, the trout in Dry Falls were beginning to recognize the TDC as a threat. That's why it wasn't working as well as it had formerly.

Other changes also were at work. The lake was beginning to suffer prolonged levels of low water, apparently from seepage through the dam at its outlet. Even during spring high water, the lake was about two feet lower than it had been historically, and in autumn months it often fell so low that some areas of the shallows nearly dried up. The lower water also made the aquatic vegetation more vulnerable to a large population of waterfowl that seemed to enjoy uprooting every plant within reach, and the combination of lower water and less vegetation erased many of the "black holes" where trout once hid. These changes also made it nearly impossible to fish a TDC, or any other fly, on a sinking line in the shallows.

These problems persist. No funds have been available to repair the dam so there is little prospect of a return to normal water levels. Several years of drought have made things even worse. Together, the changes have conspired to make the TDC a less effective fly in Dry Falls Lake than it once was.

WHEN A FAVORITE FLY STOPS WORKING, something has to be done about it. Sometimes the answer is to change the appearance of the fly, and I began experimenting with changes to the TDC. I tried adding a black marabou tail to give the fly more of an illusion of movement in the water, then substituted a wingcase of brown pheasant rump for the black thorax of the original and tried gold and copper ribbing instead of silver. Each version caught fish but none caught any more than the original TDC; something else was needed.

Thinking about the problem, I realized that during the years the TDC was so effective I had nearly always fished it under the surface with a slow retrieve; perhaps it was the fly's movement, and not the fly itself, that was now causing trout to shy away. If so, then perhaps a pattern intended to imitate a chironomid pupa hanging motionless from the surface film, waiting to hatch, would be an acceptable alternative.

That approach, however, would mean coming up with something different from a conventional TDC, which has no buoyant material. A fly designed to float more or less perpendicularly, head up and tail down, had to have something to keep it afloat. It also had to be light enough so that its total weight would not overcome its buoyancy. All this would require a delicate combination of materials.

To save weight, I decided to use a No. 14 or No. 16 3X fine-wire dry-fly hook. To add buoyancy, I opted for a deerhair overlay (shellback) over the thorax of the fly. The hollow deerhair not only would provide buoyancy, but the tips could be flared around the hook eye and trimmed to simulate the gills of a natural chironomid pupa; this would replace the ostrich herl in the original TDC.

That left the body and thorax. The body had to have enough mass to hang down from the surface film but it couldn't weigh enough to overcome the buoyancy of the deer hair. Most of the materials I tried turned out to be too heavy, so I finally ended up compromising with an extended body consisting of a single strand of black nylon wool coated with epoxy. The wool was tied so it extended about three-eighths of an inch beyond the bend of the hook; epoxy was then applied to bind the individual wool fibers in place and provide the body with enough mass so it would hang below the surface film. The compromise was that, unlike the natural, the body had no ribbing or segmentation, but I couldn't think of a way to solve that problem without adding too much weight to the fly.

Black nylon wool also was used for the thorax. A small bunch of white or pale brown deerhair was tied in at the rear of the thorax and pulled forward over the top to form the overlay and tied off behind the eye. Then the tips of the hair were flared in circular fashion around the eye of the hook and trimmed short to simulate the gills. The resulting pattern hooked a few fish, but I used it sparingly at first because it was an improbable-looking thing and I still lacked confidence in it.

All that changed early one May morning. There had been a good chironomid hatch the day before, but nothing much seemed to be happening on this particular morning. The weather was breezy, which usually holds down the hatch and makes it hard to see cruising fish in the shallows of Dry Falls. I started fishing with a TDC but had no action; other patterns also brought no interest, so I finally tied on the experimental pupa imitation and began casting to the few fish I could see feeding in the chop.

Action came immediately and I discovered that if I could spot a cruising trout and get my fly in front of it, the trout would take it almost every time. Getting the fly in front of a trout was the easy part, however; seeing it afterward was much more difficult. With most of the fly hidden below the surface, it was hard to see exactly where it was in the chop—and if I couldn't see the fly when a trout took it, I was usually unable to set the hook in time. Sometimes that proved to be the case even when I did see the take; trout took the fly willingly all day, but I managed to set the hook in only seven of them and landed only six of those.

The good news was that apparently I had found a pattern the trout would take almost without reservation; the bad news was that I couldn't seem to hook them when they did. Further experimentation revealed why: I was striking too soon. When a trout approached the fly and gently kissed the surface to suck it in, and the whole process was readily visible, it required almost more will power than I possessed to keep from setting the hook right away. But I found that if I could will myself to wait until the trout had turned away before I tried to set the hook, the number of solid hook-ups increased dramatically.

Since the new pattern was designed to float suspended in the surface film, I christened it (not very imaginatively) the "Chironomid Suspender." It quickly became my go-to fly for Dry Falls Lake. It was especially lethal on calm, bright days when trout could be seen cruising and it was possible to cast in front of them; it was also much easier to see the fly under those conditions. The pattern was less effective on windy days because both trout and fly were more difficult to see; the wind also frequently blew a belly in the floating line that made it difficult to set the hook in a taking fish. But even on breezy days the Chironomid Suspender sometimes worked well fished on a short line to partly compensate for the effects of the wind.

I was vastly pleased with the success of the new pattern, but I thought there was still room for improvement. One problem was that the pattern was slow and difficult to tie. Deerhair is hard to handle even on a large hook; trying to make it behave properly on a No. 16 fine-wire hook seemed a peculiar form of torture. Not only that, but deerhair is brittle and breaks or tears easily, and sometimes a single trout was enough to destroy a brand-new fly that might have taken twenty minutes to tie. The epoxy-coated extended wool body wasn't very durable either; after several fish, the nylon wool fibers would separate and the body would become a mere wisp of material, and after that the fly would no longer float properly in the surface film. Finally, there was the still-unsolved problem of no ribbing on the body.

I began trying different materials, mostly synthetics, in an effort to correct some of these faults. Several years of experimentation followed before I finally hit on a combination that not only solved the problems but also made the fly much easier to tie. For the extended body, I replaced the wool with a short strip of translucent clear V-Rib or Body Glass in the smallest sizes. The ribbing problem was solved by marking each section of V-Rib or Body Glass with a fine-tipped black indelible pen. The result was a translucent extended body with an extremely realistic segmented appearance and just enough weight to assure the fly would hang down from the surface film—but not enough to compromise its buoyancy.

The deerhair overlay was replaced with light brown, closed-cell foam, tied in exactly the same way as the deerhair; the foam provides just as much buoyancy and is much easier to handle than deerhair. It can't be flared around the eye of the hook like deerhair, but it can be trimmed to leave little nubbins that simulate the gills of the chironomid natural just as well as deerhair.

Perhaps best of all, these new materials are extremely durable, and now it's possible to catch fish all day on only a single fly. The pattern is still difficult to see in the water, but that's just the nature of the beast.

THE SUCCESS OF THIS "REVISED EDITION" of the Chironomid Suspender left only a single gap in my lineup of chironomid imitations: I still needed an effective imitation of newly emerged chironomid adults or egg-laying females. For years I had experimented with a series of dry-fly patterns intended to serve this purpose, mostly simple flies with floss bodies and palmered hackles, some also with deerhair wings. All took the occasional fish, but they seemed to get more refusals than takes.

One difficulty was that these flies didn't float very well; the floss bodies became waterlogged quickly, especially if the fly was skated over the surface to imitate an egg-laying female chironomid. Another problem was that they just weren't very realistic in appearance, an observation borne out by the large number of refusals. A different approach obviously was needed and I spent many hours watching trout feeding on the surface of Dry Falls until I finally saw something I thought might offer an answer.

Most of the hatching adult chironomids appeared to be taken by trout immediately after emerging from their pupal shucks, often while the empty shucks were still attached. The flies I had been using had no tails, and it occurred to me that a pattern with a tail that imitated an empty pupal shuck might work. I chose teal breast feathers for the purpose; their vivid black-and-white barred markings seemed a good representation of the segmented shuck of a real chironomid pupa.

I had also noted in my observations that while many newly hatched adult chironomids have gray bodies, a surprising number are pale yellow or sometimes almost peach in color, especially immediately after hatching (the colors seem to fade after the insects have been exposed to air for a while). So I decided to tie some flies with yellow bodies as well as gray, using palmered grizzly hackle for both. The problem of buoyancy also still had to be considered, and to solve that I decided to use the same type of deerhair overlay I had used in the original Chironomid Suspender pattern.

Putting all these ingredients together on a No. 14 3X-fine dry-fly hook, I came up with a pattern I thought looked promising. I took a few out on the lake one morning to give them a try.

Dry Falls is one of those lakes that likes to sleep late, so at first there was no sign of hatching insects or feeding fish. Then, shortly after 9 a.m., a few chironomid adults began to appear on the calm surface and occasionally a hungry trout knifed through the surface film to take one. Soon more flies began hatching and more trout began rising. I tied one of the gray-bodied emerger patterns to the end of a two-pound-test tippet and began covering rises.

The first thing I noticed was that the new fly floated much better than any of its predecessors. The second was that I began catching trout almost right away, and continued catching them all morning.

About noon a terrific hatch of damselfly nymphs came on—one of the best I'd seen. Trout usually feed very selectively during a heavy damselfly emergence, but this time, to my amazement, they continued taking the new chironomid pattern along with the natural damselfly nymphs. Later, after the damsels disappeared, the chironomids continued to hatch and the trout continued to take my new fly. When I finally quit fishing at 4 p.m., I had hooked thirty trout and landed twenty—numbers like those of the old days. But unlike the old days, these trout averaged about two pounds and several weighed nearly twice that much. Of the ten fish I lost, most had gotten into the weeds and snapped the slender two-pound tippet.

I was elated, to say the least, and hoped I had finally found a reliable imitation of the emerging adult. Subsequent experiences proved this to be the case; the pattern not only worked when fished motionless to imitate an emerging adult, but also when skated across the surface to match the movements of an egg-laying female (the trout didn't seem to notice that the skated fly had a tail, which the naturals lacked). I also found that the yellow-bodied version frequently was more effective than the gray, even when adults of both colors were on the water.

I christened this fly (again without much imagination) the Chironomid Emerger. Later I learned that Brian Chan, well-known British Columbia fisheries biologist and fly fisher, had independently developed a very similar pattern called the Lady McConnel. Chan ties his only with a gray body and uses grizzly hackle fibers instead of teal for the tail, but those are just about the only differences between the two patterns.

Recently I have started using closed-cell foam for the overlay in the Chironomid Emerger, for the same reasons I originally started using it in the Chironomid Suspender—and with similar results. During the past few years I have fished both the Suspender and Emerger patterns all over the Pacific Northwest and they have taken trout everywhere I've used them.

Best of all, they work all season long.

THESE PATTERNS, AND MANY OTHERS, are the products of an evolution that began more than four decades ago when Dick Thompson created the first TDC in a vise mounted on the steering wheel of his 1959 Rambler. Along with the new patterns have come innovative tactics for fishing them.

Considering all this, it's probably no exaggeration to say that the TDC has influenced modern Northwest fly fishing more than any other single fly pattern. Without doubt, Dick Thompson got it right the first time.

4

SALMON CANDY

(STAGE 2)

Hook: No. 8 3X fine wire

Tying thread: Tan or beige Monocord

Body: Dark green wool, very thin

Hackle: Chocolate brown, thin, palmered over front half of body
and trimmed underneath to form an inverted "V"

Tail and overlay: Dark brown deerhair, tied in at the rear of the hook
so the tips form a very short tail, then brought forward in an overlay
(shellback) and tied in just behind the eye, leaving a small topknot

IN EVERY FISHERMAN'S LIFE there are a few days that loom larger in memory than all others, days when the fishing was nearly too good to be true. The first time I fished Oregon's Hosmer Lake I had one of those days.

"There are simply not enough superlatives to describe the fishing experienced this day," I wrote afterward in my angling diary. "Suffice to say, everything that has been said and written about Hosmer is true—and then some."

Plenty has been said and written about Hosmer Lake since that day more than thirty years ago, and I've contributed my share. But I still like to turn back to that diary entry every now and then to re-read it; it brings back some of the excitement I felt that enchanted day.

I had only the one day to fish. Usually, when you're fishing new water for the first time, that's not enough time to figure out what's going on. But this time I had been well coached in advance by my old friend Ed Foss, who had plenty of fishing experience on Hosmer Lake. He told me exactly where to go and what fly to use when I got there.

So it was with more than usual confidence that I started rowing up the half-mile channel that connects the lower and upper parts of Hosmer Lake. Hosmer is really two bodies of water; the lower lake is shallow and filled with heavy weed growth that makes it difficult to see fish. The upper lake, accessible via a long, winding channel, is even shallower, but has a pumice bottom with little weed growth, a combination that often makes it possible to see cruising fish at great distances. The two lakes are so different it's hard to believe they are part of the same system.

The first thing I did when I reached the upper lake was pause to admire the incredible scenery. Ed had told me it was a beautiful spot, but his description didn't prepare me for what I saw: A broad expanse of clear, shallow water surrounded by meadows aflame with blooming bog laurel, the whole scene rimmed by magnificent mountains cloaked in shrouds of snow. "Breathaking" is a cliché, but that's exactly what it was; the view actually took my breath away. It does to this day.

I could have spent hours admiring the view, but there was other business at hand, so I went looking for the small island where Ed had told me to fish. When I found it there were large caddisflies hatching all around, and every now and then one would disappear in a big, splashy rise—the kind of rise only a sizable fish can make. These were not fish one ordinarily would expect to find in the Pacific Northwest; they were Atlantic salmon, transplanted from Gaspé Bay, Quebec, to this spectacular lake high in the Oregon Cascades.

Ed had told me to use a fly called the Salmon Candy, which he said was a good imitation of the caddisflies in Hosmer Lake. The fly, a concoction of wool, deerhair and hackle, was the creation of Lloyd Frese, a Bend, Oregon, resident who had been fishing Hosmer for years. I thought the pattern looked rather odd, but I knew from experience that Ed's advice in such matters was sound, so I had tied a dozen before my trip.

The Salmon Candy worked like a charm. In the air-clear water it was possible to see salmon approaching from great distances, then cast ahead of them and wait with mounting excitement as the fish drew near. When a fish saw the floating Salmon Candy it almost invariably rose gracefully to suck it in, and when I set the hook the fish reacted immediately. Its first response was usually a long, reel-sizzling run across the shallow flats followed by several spectacular leaps. The first run often was followed by a second and sometimes even a third or fourth, and usually there were many more jumps before the fish finally calmed down. Then it would doggedly circle the boat, fighting with apparently limitless endurance until it could no longer resist the pressure of the rod and I could lead it to the net.

Or perhaps it would be more accurate to say that's what happened after I learned not to set the hook too quickly. I discovered the hard way that when a salmon rose and took the fly, it was necessary to wait until the fish started back down before trying to set the hook; otherwise the fly would invariably come away. So each time a fish rose to my fly I forced myself to count—a thousand and one, a thousand and two, a thousand and three—before trying to set the hook. That worked, but it took all the will power I had. And I soon lost track of how many fish I had risen and hooked, except that both numbers were large.

I did keep track of the number I landed and released, and the total was seventeen. Each fish was a thing of beauty; their backs, which looked brown in the water, appeared steel-blue when they were lifted in the net, and their silver sides flashed with iridescent red-and-blue highlights. Their bellies were as white as the snow on the surrounding peaks and their flanks wore a fine spray of little X-shaped spots. Eight of the fish I landed exceeded twenty inches in length; the largest measured twenty-three. One made eight clean jumps; another ran fully twenty yards into the backing. In my excitement and clumsiness I broke off several large fish, and by day's end I had lost most of the Salmon Candy flies I had brought.

I knew I had to tie more, for after the wonderful fishing I had experienced that day, nothing could keep me from returning to Hosmer Lake.

LLOYD FRESE DIDN'T LOOK LIKE AN ACCOUNTANT. His round, weather-beaten face was creased from a lifetime's worth of grins and he spoke with a relaxed drawl that hinted of Southern origins. When I met him he was dressed in a striped work shirt, dark blue jeans and suspenders, an outfit that made him look as if he were on his way to work in a logging camp. In all the years I knew him I never saw him dressed any other way. I suppose he wore suits in town, while he was practicing his profession, and couldn't wait to shed them when he went fishing. I felt the same way and dressed much as he did, and I suppose I didn't look the part of a newspaper editor.

I met Lloyd the year after that first magical day I fished at Hosmer Lake. We spent considerable time on the water together and shared campfires in the evening, and Lloyd coached me in tying the Salmon Candy. He helped me choose just the right shade of olive-green wool for the body, showed me how to fashion it to just the right thickness, and guided me in selecting hackle of exactly the right color. He made suggestions about things I considered minor or had overlooked, but they were things he obviously thought important, and I tried to follow his instructions carefully.

At last came the long summer evening when he sat next to me and watched closely while I tied his pattern. He took the finished fly from my vise, held it up in the last rays of the sunset and inspected it closely. "Now you've got it," he said.

He was right; when I tied the pattern as he directed it was more deadly than ever. That was not surprising; the Salmon Candy was the product of many hours of careful observation Lloyd had made of the caddis hatches on Hosmer Lake. The pattern I was tying was actually one of four he had crafted to imitate various stages of the caddis-fly's life cycle.

The first two of these, which he called Stages 1 and 2, were designed to take advantage of the fact that caddis pupae in Hosmer Lake tend to swim in the surface film for long periods before hatching. Perhaps they do this in anticipation of the right combination of light, temperature and surface conditions before they make the transition from pupa to adult, but whatever the reason they spend more time swimming around than any caddis pupae I have seen elsewhere.

Lloyd had noticed the salmon often fed on these swimming pupae. He had designed Stage 1 of the Salmon Candy series to imitate a pupa swimming in the surface film under calm conditions. The Stage 1 pattern had a thin olive-green body, short tail of sparse deerhair, small deerhair collar, and a few turns of chocolate brown hackle trimmed very short.

Stage 2, the pattern I learned to tie (and the one shown at the beginning of this chapter), was similar except it had a longer deerhair overlay, stretching the full length of the fly's body; it also had a longer hackle. It was designed to imitate a swimming caddis when there was a slight chop on the water, as there is much of the time at Hosmer Lake. The deerhair overlay gave it greater buoyancy than Stage 1, and with the application of a little dry-fly dope the Stage 2 could even be "walked" or skated over the surface.

Stage 3 was intended to imitate an adult caddis in the first moments after hatching. It featured the same olive-green body—this time without a tail—a short deerhair wingcase just covering the thorax, a deerhair wing, and a hackle of mixed brown and grizzly. The deerhair was tied in just behind the eye of the hook with butts facing forward; these were trimmed short to form a sort of topknot extending over the eye of the hook. The rest of the hair was then pulled back and tied off behind the thorax, leaving the long tips extending upward and back at about a forty-five-degree angle to form the wing.

Stage 4 was designed to imitate a recently emerged adult or a female returning to the surface to lay eggs. It had the same olive-green body, a full, thick deerhair wing and a hackle of mixed brown and grizzly. With judicious application of dry-fly dope, it could be skated over the surface to imitate the skittering movements of a newly hatched adult or an egg-laying female.

The Stage 2 was the most popular, not just with me but with many other fishermen. The reason was obvious: The Stage 2 worked so well the other patterns were rarely needed. When a hatch was in progress, or about to begin, a Stage 2 Salmon Candy cast in front of a cruising salmon would almost always bring a spectacular, splashing rise. The fly worked nearly as well even when there was no hatch; the salmon, apparently remembering the appearance of the naturals, would continue taking the Salmon Candy avidly even several days after the last caddis hatch had ended.

MY FISHING DIARY INCLUDES MANY ACCOUNTS of twenty-, thirty-, even fifty-fish days at Hosmer Lake on the Salmon Candy. Not all days were that productive, of course; for a number of reasons, the salmon population in the lake varied dramatically from one year to the next. Some years it was impossible to catch twenty fish a day because there were hardly that many in the lake. But even during lean years, the Salmon Candy usually brought fish of a size and quality to compensate for lack of numbers.

I remember one cold, misty, late-June morning when a magnificent salmon rose to my fourth cast of the day and gracefully swallowed my Salmon Candy. It made three magnificent leaps and three trips into the backing before its first flush of strength was spent. After that came many shorter runs until the fish finally grew tired enough that I could lead it alongside my boat and measure it against my rod. I removed the fly from its mouth, doffed my hat, and watched the salmon swim away; when it was gone I took a tape measure and stretched it along my rod to the point I had marked; the distance was twenty-six inches.

Less than a half hour later I hooked another salmon that appeared even larger. A big buck, it made a magnificent leap followed by so many long runs I lost count. At last it settled down to duke it out at close quarters and the battle became an endurance contest. Twice the fish went under my boat and I had to pass the rod under the anchor rope to keep it from getting fouled. Several times I tried to bring the fish to the surface, but my light fly rod was unequal to the task. Only when the salmon came to the surface on its own, exhausted, was I able to lead it to the net. Then I discovered the net was too small; the fish wouldn't fit inside the rim. On the third try, I managed to get the salmon's nose into the mesh and scoop it up with its tail hanging far over the other side of the net. It measured slightly more than twenty-seven inches.

The fly that took both fish—a badly chewed-up Salmon Candy—is still taped to the page in my fishing diary that describes another one of the best days I ever had.

There have been other days nearly as memorable. Once a big salmon rose to a floating Salmon Candy next to my little nine-foot boat, rocketed out of the water, and fell into the boat right at my feet. Before I could react, the fish somehow propelled itself back over the side into the water and swam away. Another time a big salmon took my Salmon Candy, made a dash for shore, jumped out of the water into thick grass growing along the lake's edge, thrashed around in the grass until it broke the leader, then flopped back in the water and disappeared.

One year, the average size of the salmon in Hosmer was quite small. Thinking it would be more fun if I matched my tackle to the size of the fish, I went out on the lake one morning with a five-foot midge rod rigged with a three-weight line and a Hardy Featherweight reel too small to accommodate any backing. Of course the first salmon I saw was the largest I'd seen on the whole trip; it came to my third cast and took the Salmon Candy with a confident slurp.

I set the hook and the salmon leaped high in the air, then started a run that made the little Featherweight shriek. I held my breath and watched while the fish took line until bare metal was showing through the last few remaining turns. But luck was on my side; the fish stopped in the nick of time and I managed to recover some of the line before it started a second run. Once more it stopped just short of spooling me, and after that we went through the whole business a third time. By then the fish was tiring and its runs were getting shorter. At length it surrendered—a thick, handsome fish that taped out at twenty-five inches and probably weighed about five pounds. It turned out to be the best fish of the trip.

After my initial experiences with the Salmon Candy, I couldn't wait to try it during some of the spectacular traveling sedge hatches on the Kamloops trout lakes of British Columbia. It worked just as well there as it had at Hosmer. It was a Salmon Candy that took my first trout during the filming of a segment of the "American Sportsman" show for the ABC Television Network (along with that catch, I noted in my fishing diary that the show's producer was handing out Cuban cigars that cost $1.40 each, which seemed to me an absolutely outrageous sum for a cigar—but that was more than twenty-five years ago).

Roche Lake was one of the British Columbia waters where I was especially anxious to try the Salmon Candy. Sometimes, during spring high water, big trout would cruise the channels between beds of *chara* weed at Roche Lake's south end. Usually they were wary and there were not very many of them, but they would come into the shallows to feed on sedge pupae rising from the *chara* weed. The first time I used the Salmon Candy for this fishing, I landed ten fish up to five pounds during three days of intensely interesting fishing.

The Salmon Candy also worked well at Lundbom, Hihium, Valentine and other British Columbia lakes noted for their sedge hatches. In fact, it worked well wherever I fished during hatches of large caddisflies or sedges.

ONE YEAR, A CALIFORNIA ATTORNEY named Dave Draheim and his family camped next to us at Hosmer Lake. We struck up an acquaintance that was renewed the following year and the year after that until our two families began looking forward to a spring rendezvous at Hosmer Lake as if it were an annual holiday. Eventually our growing friendship inspired Dave and me to travel to other waters—Washington steelhead rivers, British Columbia lakes, New Brunswick's Miramichi River, even Christmas Island in the far Pacific. But our annual meeting at Hosmer Lake became almost an institution, and it has continued now for three decades.

During that time there have been only two or three occasions when circumstances kept us from fishing together at Hosmer. One year Dave was forced to delay his trip until two weeks after mine; afterward he sent me a letter describing a strange experience.

Dave had been taking his young son for a boat ride on the lake when he saw an osprey plunge into the water and emerge with a large salmon in its talons. The osprey struggled to rise from the surface but was unable to gain altitude and finally had to drop the salmon, which fell back into the water not far from Dave's boat. The fish was still alive but apparently in difficulty, so Dave rowed over to see if he could help it.

The salmon was bleeding from several puncture wounds caused by the osprey's talons, but these were not necessarily fatal; fish with scars from healed talon punctures are common in Hosmer Lake. But the salmon also was in respiratory distress from having been out of the water, so Dave grasped it and started moving it gently back and forth through the water, trying to restore circulation through its gills. Soon a throb of life returned to the fish and he let go and watched it swim away.

Rowing away from the scene, Dave looked back and noticed the salmon again had floated to the surface, belly-up, so he turned around and started back to see what more he could do. This time, when he grasped the salmon for another attempt at resuscitation, he noticed a fly stuck in its jaw. He twisted the fly free, placed it in his boat, then made another attempt to get the salmon going. As before, the fish eventually revived, swam away and this time disappeared.

Only then did Dave take a close look at the fly he had removed from the fish. It was a Salmon Candy and he thought he recognized the tying style; he enclosed the fly with his letter to see if I could verify the tyer's identity. A quick look was all I needed to identify the fly as one I had tied. I had hooked the salmon more than two weeks earlier and it had broken my leader and escaped with the fly. I wrote back to Dave, confirming his suspicion that the fly was one of mine.

I thought it a rather amazing coincidence that my friend had recovered a fly I had lost in a fish weeks earlier, but that wasn't quite the end of the story. Two years later, when Dave and I again were fishing Hosmer together, I was preparing to release a salmon I had caught when I was startled to see I hadn't hooked the fish at all; instead, in a million-to-one chance, the hook of my fly had gone through the eye of a fly already stuck in the salmon's jaw. I had hooked the fly instead of the fish.

I removed both flies and let the fish go, then took a closer look at the fly that had actually been in the salmon's mouth. It was a small mayfly emerger pattern and I thought I knew who had tied it. That night, when Dave and I met in camp to compare results from the day's fishing, I showed him the fly. He identified it immediately it as one of his and said he had broken it off in a fish two days earlier.

So we were even: Each of us had found one of the other's flies stuck in a salmon's mouth. I suppose it was better to find them there than stuck in some overhanging branch.

FOR TWENTY-FIVE YEARS THE SALMON CANDY was the best fly in my arsenal, accounting for more fish than any other pattern. That might seem odd, given that caddis hatches on most waters rarely last more than a month. But that month—from early June to early July—often brought more fish than the other eleven months combined. One reason was that trout seemed to lose all inhibitions when big caddisflies were hatching. But the biggest reason was the Salmon Candy itself; it was almost infallible when a hatch was in progress.

That near infallibility caused me to ignore several things I had noticed about the Salmon Candy almost as soon as I began tying and fishing it. One was its extreme vulnerability; the deerhair overlay was fully exposed to the teeth of salmon or trout, and sometimes a single fish would shred a brand-new fly. Another was the pattern's tendency to become waterlogged and sink, especially after it had been skated over the surface for a while. The Salmon Candy also took a long time to tie, or at least it did for me, and that, combined with its high mortality rate in the mouths of fish, usually left me chronically short of Salmon Candies. No matter how many I tied before each trip, I'd run out after a few days. Tying more cut seriously into the time available for fishing.

Those problems finally prompted me to seek ways to improve the durability and floatability of the Salmon Candy and reduce the time it took to tie it. This was not something I went about in an organized or purposeful way; the original pattern worked so well I was reluctant to tinker with it. But its shortcomings were just enough of an annoyance to encourage me to experiment when I had the time and materials. For a while nothing I tried worked, and after each failed experiment I went back to tying the Salmon Candy according to Lloyd Frese's specifications.

This continued until one day I hit upon a new formula that seemed promising. I had been experimenting with an extended body for chironomid emergers, which gave me the idea that a similar approach might work with caddis emergers. An extended body would allow use of a smaller, lighter hook, which would help the fly stay afloat. The body also wouldn't have to be as long or thick as in the original Salmon Candy, and that meant it wouldn't become waterlogged as quickly. An extended body would rule out a deerhair overlay covering the full length of the fly, but a shorter overlay, just long enough to cover the thorax, might still provide enough buoyancy to keep the fly afloat. It would also be less vulnerable to trout or salmon teeth.

With these thoughts in mind, I tied a couple of experimental patterns with extended bodies. I used the same dark olive nylon wool I had always used to tie the Salmon Candy, except this time the wool was twisted into a "noodle." The ends of the "noodle" were secured near the center of a size 10 dry-fly hook; the rest was allowed to extend rearward, forming an extended body. Just forward of the "noodle" I tied in a thick bunch of deerhair and a dark brown hackle feather. The hackle was palmered forward to the eye of the hook, then trimmed on top and bottom. The final step was to bring the deerhair forward over the hackle and tie it off behind the eye, then trim the excess except for a little topknot over the eye.

The new pattern got its first test at Hosmer Lake on a June afternoon. It was a windy day, which made it difficult to see cruising or rising fish in the chop, but the new fly floated well despite the conditions. It also attracted its share of fish; I counted fourteen rises to the fly, eleven of them "blind"—meaning I didn't see the fish before it took the fly. By the time I realized what had happened it was too late to set the hook, and I missed every single rise. I saw the three other fish coming before they took the fly and hooked all three firmly. One was small—about fifteen inches—but the others were decent fish, one about eighteen inches, the other a little more than twenty.

Those results were encouraging but not enough to persuade me to stop using the original Salmon Candy pattern. They were good enough to encourage more experiments, however.

That winter Dave Draheim sent me some olive-brown mohair that I thought an even closer match for the color of Hosmer Lake caddis pupae than the dark olive nylon wool I had always used before. The mohair also looked as if it would shed water better than nylon wool, and when I twisted it into a "noodle" its natural fuzzy texture had more of a "buggy" look than the sharply defined silhouette of the wool body. So I tied several flies using mohair for the extended body and tried them at Hosmer the following spring. They worked well enough to make me tie the new pattern and the old Salmon Candy in equal numbers before my next trip.

That was in June, 1996, and the first day I fished the new pattern it took twenty-five salmon. The next day it took nineteen more. It kept on taking fish in similar numbers until I ran out of the new pattern and had to resort to my supply of original Salmon Candies.

These results satisfied me that I had finally overcome the problems with the original pattern and come up with an acceptable substitute. The new pattern was more durable, floated as well if not better than the original Salmon Candy—even when skated across the surface—and was much faster and easier to tie. Best of all, the salmon took it as avidly as they'd ever taken Lloyd Frese's original.

I haven't yet tried the new pattern in all the waters where I fished the Salmon Candy successfully, but the new fly has worked well wherever I have tried it—and it has given me some of the best fishing I've had in recent years.

It needed a name, so—again with little imagination—I christened it the Caddis Emerger. It is now my fly of choice when caddisflies are hatching, but I do not claim it as an original or innovative pattern; it owes its existence to the Salmon Candy and to Lloyd Frese's careful observations and fly-tying skills. His dressing served me extremely well for many years, and the Caddis Emerger is simply a rearrangement of most of the same materials in his original design.

I like to think of it as the Son of Salmon Candy.

FOR NEARLY A DECADE I FISHED OFTEN WITH Lloyd Frese at Hosmer Lake. But even more than fly fishing, Lloyd had a passion for training bird dogs and hunting upland game birds, so when he retired from his accounting business, he and his wife moved to a small, isolated community on the Snake River in far eastern Oregon, where the hillsides beckoned with exciting hunting opportunities. His new home was a long way from Hosmer Lake, but by then the fishing in Hosmer was already declining.

I saw him only once after that, but every year, usually in mid-winter, I would receive a large box in the mail bearing his return address. The box never weighed much and I knew before I opened it exactly what I would find inside: Neatly packed plastic bags filled with pheasant skins and carefully selected strips of dark brown deerhair, just the right shade for tying Salmon Candies. There would also be a brief note in Lloyd's handwriting: "Help yourself and share the rest."

I would pick out what I needed and take the rest to a meeting of the Washington Fly Fishing Club, of which Lloyd was an associate member; there the pheasant skins and deerhair strips would disappear quickly into the pockets of other fly tyers. Then I would write Lloyd a note to acknowledge receipt of the shipment and thank him for the latest of what we came to call his annual "CARE packages."

Then one year no package came. Nor did one arrive the following year, or the year after that. Notes to Lloyd went unanswered.

I remember it was Lloyd Frese who once told me he feared dying because he was worried heaven couldn't possibly be as good as Hosmer Lake.

Perhaps now he knows the answer.

5

TARBOO SPECIAL

(MODERN VERSION)

Hook: No. 4 3XL stainless-steel ring-eye hook or No. 4 3XL
turned-up eye Atlantic salmon hook (black finish)

Tying thread: Black

Body and tail: Medium silver braided Mylar tubing with core
removed, bound to hook shank fore and aft. Leave about a half
inch of tubing behind at the rear and pick out individual strands
of Mylar braid to form the tail

Underwing: White or cream polar bear hair or substitute, tied sparsely

Overwing: Dyed green or mixed green and blue polar bear hair or
substitute, with several strands of Krystal Flash in matching colors

THE LETTER WAS FROM THE FLY-TYING COLUMNIST for a national outdoor magazine and he wanted me to send him a pattern he could feature in his monthly column. It was a flattering request, but it left me wondering how to respond.

I had precious few fly patterns to my credit and most of those were my own private dressings, otherwise unknown; not only that, but I was hesitant to share the results of my awkward fly-tying skills with someone who wrote about flies for a living, let alone with a national audience.

But I thought about it a while and finally decided I would send the columnist a pattern I had developed for winter sea-run cutthroat fishing in the estuaries of Puget Sound and Hood Canal. At the time this was a very specialized local fishery, shared by a small clan of diehard anglers, and I thought it unlikely either the columnist or most of his audience would have seen a fly tied for winter sea-run cutthroat fishing. That being so, perhaps they would be more inclined to overlook the shortcomings of the pattern I decided to send.

It was a fly called the Tarboo Special, named after Tarboo Bay, a place I fished often. It had been conceived as an imitation of the three-spine stickleback that is an important seasonal food for cutthroat in some Puget Sound and Hood Canal estuaries, but had since evolved to become more of an all-purpose forage-fish pattern.

The particular example I selected to send to the columnist was the best I could find in my assortment of sea-run cutthroat flies. As with most of my patterns it was far from perfect; the head, especially, looked awkward and uneven. I fully expected that once the columnist saw it he would throw it away and look elsewhere for a pattern for his column.

So I was very much surprised when the magazine appeared with his column featuring the Tarboo Special. "I spent a good deal of time looking at the Tarboo Special before finally selecting it for the column," the columnist wrote. I could well imagine that but his next words amazed me: "The more I looked at it, the more I admired Steve Raymond's design. I expect to incorporate a number of the fly's features in my own streamer patterns."

Design? What design? I had needed a pattern to serve as a baitfish imitation and had quickly selected materials I thought would work and lashed them to the hook. The notion that I was "designing" a fly never occurred to me. The dressing was so basic that I couldn't imagine what features the columnist could possibly want to incorporate in his own streamer patterns. But as I continued reading I found out:

"The choice of polar bear for both wing and throat gives the fly a sheen and sparkle common to the natural. The mylar tubing for the body gives the fly a 'substantial' look, which fish find attractive. The pattern's overall compactness gives it a castability that is extremely important to the coastal angler. The high winds often found along beaches force the angler to use flies with good aerodynamic properties, or he will be unable to place the cast accurately."

Oh.

Imagine that. I had managed to incorporate all these features into the Tarboo Special without even knowing it.

When I got over my surprise, I decided the whole business was rather amusing. I also had to admit it was flattering to have my mediocre work praised in such effusive terms.

But that wasn't the end of the matter. A famous angling writer saw the magazine column, picked up the pattern and published it in one of his books, along with a color illustration. Suddenly I found myself in very fast fly-tying company, where I knew I didn't belong.

Fortunately, neither the magazine column nor the book was enough to make the Tarboo Special a household name. The column was published many years ago and now even the book is out of print, and I suspect I am still the only one fishing the Tarboo Special.

THE VERSION OF THE TARBOO SPECIAL I sent to the magazine columnist was not the same as the original. Braided mylar tubing wasn't available when I tied the prototype, so I had simply fashioned the body out of flat silver tinsel wound around the hook shank. Long-shank stainless-steel hooks also were as rare as hen's teeth in those days (the 1970s), so I tied the fly on an Atlantic salmon hook with a black finish. This meant the fly usually had a short shelf life because any attempt to sharpen the hook or pinch down the barb would crack the finish and corrosion would start as soon as the fly was immersed in salt water. As a result, I could usually expect only one or two fishing trips out of each fly before I had to throw it away and tie another replacement.

The original pattern also lacked a tail. But the biggest difference between it and the one I sent to the fly-tying columnist was that the original fly incorporated a whole rainbow's worth of colored floss in the wing. Strands of gold, cerise, green, ice blue, pink, yellow and lavender floss had been cut to matching lengths and tied between the underwing and overwing; when the fly was in the water, the floss strips blended to provide a reasonable approximation of the spectrum of colors that reflect off the sides of natural baitfish (remember, this was long before the advent of materials like Krystal Flash or

Flashabou). The result, I thought, was a very handsome fly.

Others agreed. One whose judgment was especially meaningful was Syd Glasso, one of the great fly tyers of his day. Syd and I had gone sea-run cutthroat fishing together and he was watching when I took a Tarboo Special from my fly box and started to tie it on.

"Let me see that," he said.

I showed him the fly, wincing inwardly as he held it up for close inspection.

"Look at that," he said, showing the fly to a couple of other anglers who were with us. "Look what he's done with that colored floss. What a good idea!"

That was high praise from someone now remembered for his beautiful and graceful steelhead Spey flies, which are far beyond my tying capabilities.

With the multiple layers of colored floss in its wing, the Tarboo Special *was* a good-looking fly, both in and out of water. The trouble was, cutting all those floss strips and marrying them together took a lot of time, and since I was tying a lot of Tarboo Specials—replacements for those rapidly rusting away—I was always on the lookout for ways to speed the tying process. Eliminating the colored floss was one obvious way to do that; eliminating the throat that was also part of the original pattern was another. Eventually I did both.

Fortunately, that was just about the time Mylar tubing came on the market, and I started using it instead of tinsel for the body of the fly. The scale-like braided Mylar formed a bulkier, more realistic body and reflected light in different colors, so I considered it a good substitute for the colored floss; at least I convinced myself that it was. Fraying the end of the Mylar tubing also made a good tail for the fly.

That was as far as the Tarboo Special had evolved when I got the letter from the magazine columnist. Since then I have continued experimenting with the pattern and the biggest change has been to start tying it on long-shank stainless-steel hooks, now readily available. With these hooks it is possible to sharpen the point or pinch down the barb without having to worry about corrosion, and that means I no longer have to tie as many flies. Artificial hair also has replaced polar bear for the wing and a version of the fly with a red wing has proven very effective.

I also tried adding stick-on eyes to the fly's head, but the stick-on eyes never stuck, so I gave that up. Another change, however, did become permanent, and that was the addition of a few strands of Krystal Flash to match the wing color; these, I think, enhance the pattern's appearance in the water.

So that's where the Tarboo Special stands today. It has become my standard generic forage-fish imitation for sea-run cutthroat in Puget Sound, Hood Canal and elsewhere, used wherever sticklebacks, candlefish, smelt or similar species are present. It works well for all of these.

WHILE THE TARBOO SPECIAL WAS UNDERGOING ITS EVOLUTION, the sea-run cutthroat fishery also was evolving rapidly. Only a handful of anglers were involved in the sport when I began fishing for sea-run cutthroat more than thirty years ago; now there are hundreds if not thousands. This has both helped and hurt the fishery.

On the positive side, the growing number of anglers has helped call attention to the plight of sea-run cutthroat, which are among the last wild trout remaining in the Pacific Northwest. Populations of these fish were declining rapidly almost everywhere until pressure from burgeoning ranks of sea-run cutthroat anglers finally forced Washington State to adopt catch-and-release regulations. These had an almost immediate positive impact on both numbers and average size of sea-run cutthroat in Puget Sound and Hood Canal, and the fishing now is better than it has been for years.

On the downside, the once secret, sacred spots where cutthroat anglers used to fish in solitude must now be shared with others— and the catch must be shared as well. What was once almost a private fishery has become very public indeed, and now there is competition for both space on the water and for the fish inhabiting that space. At least regulations now require the release of those fish so they can survive to spawn, and perhaps be caught again, and I suppose popularization of the fishery is not an unreasonable price to pay for such protection.

Nevertheless, I miss the old days. Maybe I'm just showing my age, but I fondly remember when Puget Sound sea-run cutthroat anglers were such a small group that nearly everybody knew everybody else by his first name. We fished mostly during the winter, and in the rainy provinces of the Pacific Northwest it's not unusual for a winter angler to be almost as wet as the fish he is trying to catch.

The rain begins in November, when a perpetual overcast settles down to treetop level and bleaches away all the color; everything turns gray and remains that way, with rare exceptions, until late March or early April. Yet that's prime cutthroat weather; the sea-run cutthroat, whose natural range is defined almost exactly by the limits of the Pacific coastal rainforests, is most at home in a wet, dark world. If you want to catch them, it means you have to go out in the dark and the wet.

So that's what we did, spending many long, wet, fishless hours looking for places where sea-run cutthroat could reliably be found.

There are not many of these, because the sea-run is a highly site-specific fish. Nobody knows exactly why, but sea-runs often prefer to congregate in one small spot to the exclusion of dozens of others that look exactly the same. Once one of these spots is discovered, an angler can return to it with assurance he will find fish there again and again. Such information is considered of great value, to be shared only with trusted friends.

One of the most reliable spots was near the "toe" of Hood Canal, a giant boot-shaped saltwater fjord that runs north-south over most of its length, then makes a nearly right-angle turn northeast toward the little town of Belfair, which lies at the very tip of the boot's toe. Many small creeks flow into this section of Hood Canal and nearly all have spawning populations of sea-run cutthroat. The trout were the main attraction for anglers, but a popular secondary attraction was a ramshackle establishment known as Harold's North Shore Inn, situated on the beach almost exactly in the center of the best fishing area.

After a morning of fishing, it was not unusual for several cold, wet anglers to run their boats up on the beach in front of Harold's and go inside to warm up in front of the large fireplace. The fireplace was usually stoked with green alder that sputtered and sparked and smoked heavily, but even the wet wood broadcast welcome heat and it was common to see three or four dripping-wet anglers clustered around the reluctant fire. Harold's also featured beer on tap and wonderfully greasy hamburgers, so anglers could slake their thirst and satisfy their hunger while they warmed up and dried off.

There were, however, some unspoken rules that had to be observed. Fly fishers from the big city, as most of us were, needed to be careful what they said at Harold's because most of the other patrons were local out-of-work loggers, many missing a few teeth or a couple of fingers, and they held strong opinions about city-dwelling tree-huggers and the like. They gathered at Harold's on Saturdays to watch football, drink beer, talk dirty and spend their unemployment checks, then went home to beat their wives. Despite the great differences in our backgrounds and world views, we big-city fly fishers got along pretty well with them, possibly because we were always dressed much as they were—quilted plaid shirts, heavy pants worn over long underwear, ankle-high boots, and massive, shapeless, waterproof parkas. When people are dressed alike and drink the same beer, it's amazing how they all end up more or less on the same wavelength. Maybe that's a recipe for peace in the Middle East.

After warming up, devouring a hamburger and downing two or three beers for lunch, it was always advisable for anglers to relieve themselves in the men's room at Harold's before they ventured back out on the water. One day I found myself standing in line for what seemed the longest time, waiting a turn at the urinal. The guy at the front of the line kept fumbling endlessly with his clothes; finally he admitted his problem: "The trouble is, I've got five inches of clothes on and my dick is only three inches long."

That got a big laugh. It was the kind of humor you expected at Harold's.

Sometimes, after lunch, we would go outside to find the tide had gone out, leaving our boats high and dry on the beach. Then we would have to drag the boats over a wide expanse of clinging, near-ly bottomless mud to reach the water. This was a dirty, difficult job, usually accompanied by much heavy cursing. The mud was a formidable obstacle by itself, but after two or three beers it became even more so, and on several occasions I witnessed slightly inebriated fly fishers go face down in the muck. It never happened to me, although I came close a few times.

Most of us also carried brandy flasks in our boats. This was necessary, we told one another, so an antidote would be available in case we were bitten by marauding sea serpents, but the real reason was to have something we could use to brace ourselves on extra-cold mornings when we couldn't wait to get in front of the fireplace at Harold's.

One day a member of our group got an early start on his flask and was already pretty well lubricated by the time we adjourned to Harold's for lunch. He downed several beers during lunch, then returned to his skiff and went to work on the remaining contents of his flask. By midafternoon he was a hazard to navigation, and I watched in horror as he throttled up his outboard and headed at high speed for a nearby dock. He had gone under the dock several hours earlier with plenty of room to spare, but the tide had risen several feet since then; now, unless he remembered to duck, it didn't look as if he would make it. Oblivious to the approaching danger and unable to hear our shouts over the noise of his outboard, he sped under the dock with head held high—and the dock took his hat off. Another inch and it would have been his head.

It was obvious he was in no shape to continue on his own, so the rest of us converged on his skiff and made him sit in the bow while another angler took over steering and headed for a nearby boat ramp. They were still twenty-five feet from shore when our lubricated friend, trying to be helpful, took the skiff's bow rope in hand and stepped over the side into four feet of water. By the time we got him out of the water and into the back seat of somebody's station wagon, he was snoring blissfully.

That sort of thing didn't happen very often, thank goodness. But we had a lot of fun at Harold's North Shore Inn. Sometimes the fishing was good, too.

It's all different now. Harold's Inn has changed hands several times and I haven't gone back there since one of the newer owners installed a gift shop—a gift shop!—with dolls and doilies and other feminine-type things. Most of the fishing companions with whom I spent those happy days also have since gone to fish in other waters, and while the younger anglers who have taken their place are all good fellows, they don't share the memories I have. They listen politely to my stories, but I guess you had to be there to appreciate them. Realizing that makes me feel old.

But not so old that I can't still cast a Tarboo Special and catch a few sea-run cutthroat. And there are still plenty in Hood Canal to be caught.

MONOFILAMENT FLY LINES WERE BUT A GLEAM in some manufacturer's eye when I began fishing the Tarboo Special, so I used a sink-tip line instead. It worked well enough most of the time, but the combined forces of wind and tide sometimes made the floating portion of the line move faster than the sinking tip, and this produced a hinged effect that made it difficult to detect strikes or set the hook in a fish. So when the first intermediate (slow-sinking) monofilament fly lines came on the market, I was quick to try them for sea-run cutthroat fishing.

The intermediate lines worked much better. To my mind, they were ideally suited for cutthroat fishing because they eliminated the hinge effect and made it possible to control the depth of the fly. Sea-run cutthroat in estuaries often feed in very shallow water, but with an intermediate line it was possible to cast a Tarboo Special into water only a few inches deep, start retrieving immediately, and fish the fly just under the surface. In situations where fish were holding in deeper water, it was necessary only to wait a few seconds for the line to sink the fly to the proper depth, then begin the retrieve. The intermediate monofilament lines were far more versatile than a sink-tip, and I have been using them ever since.

Sea-run cutthroat are not the only species I have taken on the Tarboo Special. Once I got an early start celebrating New Year's Eve by visiting Tarboo Bay on the twenty-ninth of December. It was a dark, overcast day and a strong north wind was sweeping down the bay, piling up whitecaps. I could see at once that fishing would be difficult, but decided to hazard it anyway. I launched my cartop boat and fished through the late morning on an outgoing tide, trying to time my casts between gusts. For the first couple of hours I had no strikes and saw only a single cutthroat jump—and that one wasn't attached to my fly.

Then I saw what I thought was another cutthroat leap out of the broken water a short distance away. I rowed to the spot, cast into the swiftly moving tidal current and let the fly swing around in the same fashion one would fish a fly downstream in a steelhead river. The fly was halfway through the swing when I felt the pull of a good fish. It fought briskly without jumping and turned out to be a fat young blackmouth, or chinook salmon. I released it, resumed casting and soon had another strike that turned out to be a second chinook, slightly larger than the first. Then the wind became even stronger and I was finally forced to head ashore—but the Tarboo Special had accounted for another species.

Another time, while fishing near Belfair, I had already caught and released several cutthroat on a Tarboo Special when I saw a rise from what I thought was probably another sea-run. I cast toward the spot, dropping the Tarboo Special amid the rings still spreading from the rise, and felt a good take almost immediately. The fish was strong and fought deep, never jumping, and when I finally coaxed it to the surface I was surprised to see it wasn't a cutthroat but a dusky sea perch, fat and silvery and weighing about one and one-half pounds. I had caught sea perch on other flies but never on a forage-fish pattern; chalk up another species for the Tarboo Special.

Since then the Tarboo Special also has accounted for coho salmon, sea-run Dolly Varden, steelhead and starry flounder, confirming my judgment that it is a good, all-around baitfish imitation wherever estuarine fish are found.

I HAVE ALWAYS FISHED ESTUARIES for sea-run cutthroat in the winter, and other anglers were doing so long before I started. So it came as quite a surprise to all of us when we learned fisheries biologists had declared there *are* no cutthroat in the estuaries during winter. The reason, they said, is that cutthroat spend winters in fresh water.

This isn't the first time biologists have been wrong. But rarely have they been so stubbornly, persistently wrong, especially in the face of irrefutable evidence to the contrary.

The fact is that many cutthroat *do* spend their winters in fresh water—many, but not all. Throughout its natural range, from California's Eel River to Prince William Sound, Alaska, the sea-run cutthroat has adopted many different life-history strategies to meet the requirements of many different environments. It is, perhaps, the ultimate pragmatist among fish, certainly among salmonids, always finding ways to get along and assure survival of the species.

Many of these life-history strategies have been documented by scientists—many, but not all. One of the first studies of sea-run cutthroat, by the biologist R. D. Giger, concluded that Oregon coastal cutthroat always winter in fresh water, never in the salt. This oft-cited study seems to have led succeeding generations of biologists to assume that what is true for Oregon coastal cutthroat must be true for all cutthroat. Given the wide variety of cutthroat life histories that have been documented, this is a dangerous assumption to make—and in fact it is wrong.

But it persists. No less an authority than Robert J. Behnke, generally considered the world's foremost expert on trout, declared in a recent book that the sea-run cutthroat "typically spends only two or three months in salt water" and that all sea-runs "return to fresh water for overwintering." Considering Behnke's enormous prestige within the biological community, his statements surely will be taken at face value and repeated by other biologists, perpetuating what many anglers know to be a myth.

Don't blame Behnke; he lives in Colorado, far from the nearest sea-run cutthroat, and undoubtedly relied on the conclusions of other biologists.

The facts are these: It is almost certainly true that Oregon coastal cutthroat do spend winters in fresh water, but Oregon has a much different type of coastline than Washington, British Columbia or Alaska. Many of the rivers that flow into the Pacific Ocean along the Oregon coast are large enough to provide ample shelter; those hosting salmon runs also provide at least a temporary abundance of food in the form of loose salmon spawn during late fall and early winter. Oregon's coastal estuaries, on the other hand, are mostly small and poorly sheltered, offering little food and not much in the way of sanctuary from winter ocean storms. The violent surf stirred up by these storms creates a dangerous, hostile environment for cutthroat, so it's little wonder they have adopted a strategy of escaping to the rivers to spend the winter.

By contrast, Washington's Puget Sound and Hood Canal are well protected from winter storms, as is much of the Inside Passage along the British Columbia coast and the Alaska Panhandle. The sea-run cutthroat appears to have adopted at least two different survival strategies in these sheltered waters. Cutthroat in northern Puget Sound behave much the same way as their Oregon coastal counterparts, returning each fall or winter to large rivers such as the Nooksack, Skagit, Stillaguamish and Snohomish. All these major river systems host large salmon runs, and cutthroat apparently enter them not from any need for shelter but possibly instead to feast on the abundant salmon spawn. Once having entered the rivers for this purpose, they remain until the time comes for them to spawn themselves.

But most of the streams entering south Puget Sound and Hood Canal are small or medium-sized at best—too small to offer much in the way of food or shelter. Lacking a ready freshwater food source or a need to seek shelter from winter storms, the cutthroat in south Puget Sound and Hood Canal typically spend winters in the estuaries. This makes good sense from a survival standpoint, for even during winter the estuaries offer much more in the way of food than the small, acidic streams flowing into them.

Of course adult cutthroat must still ascend these little creeks to spawn, and they do—but usually it's a quick trip, the fish's equivalent of a one-night stand, and they return to salt water as soon as they can. Recently spawned cutthroat kelts are sometimes caught by anglers in salt water during the winter, but kelts form only a small percentage of the catch. At least ninety percent of the winter cutthroat harvested in salt water are bright fish, either maiden cutthroat yet to make their first spawning journey or "skip spawners"—fish that spawned a year earlier, then returned to salt water to remain for a whole year before spawning again.

These fish are available in large numbers throughout the estuaries of Puget Sound and Hood Canal all winter long. Based on limited fishing experience in British Columbia and Alaska, I believe the same is true in at least some of those waters. Very little research has been done on these populations, however, and their life histories mostly remain a mystery.

Anglers have known about the presence of these winter fish for at least sixty years, but biologists persist in clinging to the myth that they do not exist. Maybe that's a good thing, for it could help keep the winter sea-run cutthroat fishery from growing even more popular than it already has.

In the interests of scientific accuracy, however, I will be glad to loan a couple of Tarboo Specials to any interested biologist, take him to one of my favorite spots, and let him see for himself that some cutthroat really do spend their winters in salt water.

It was a cold day in December, but a distant sun peeked occasionally through broken clouds to light up the waters of Tarboo Bay. When it did, we could sometimes see the ghostly shapes of cutthroat feeding over the cobbled bottom. This was a treat—usually estuary fish are invisible except when they rise—and it added excitement to the fishing. Sometimes it was possible to cast to individual feeding fish, some of them quite large.

My fishing partner that day was Frank Amato, publisher of angling books, and it was his first experience fishing for sea-run cutthroat in estuaries. We had each caught several, some as large as eighteen inches—good-sized for a sea-run—and the day seemed to be going nicely. I was happy Frank was having a good introduction to this fishing.

Then the clouds closed ranks and the sun disappeared, along with the chance to see fish. The fishing slowed and after a while Frank grew tired of fishing from a boat, so he went ashore and started casting from the beach.

He hadn't been doing so very long when he heard hammering sounds close by. Looking around to locate the origin of the sounds, Frank saw a man nailing a sign to a nearby tree. He reeled in and walked over to see what the sign said.

It said: "No Trespassing."

"Does that mean me?" Frank asked.

"It sure as hell does," said the man with the hammer and nails.

So Frank returned to his boat, rowed away from the newly posted beach, and resumed fishing.

We laughed about the incident later, with no inkling that it marked the beginning of the end. Since that day many more "No Trespassing" signs have appeared around the margins of Tarboo Bay until now there is no longer any public access. Sadly, the same thing has happened in many other locations around Puget Sound and Hood Canal, closing off the once-favorite spots of many sea-run cutthroat fishermen, or at least making them very difficult to reach.

That means the remaining places have taken on even greater value and importance, and sea-run cutthroat anglers must be vigilant to assure continued access to them.

I doubt I shall ever neglect that duty. The Tarboo Special, just by its name, is a constant reminder of what already has been lost.

6

GOLDEN SHRIMP

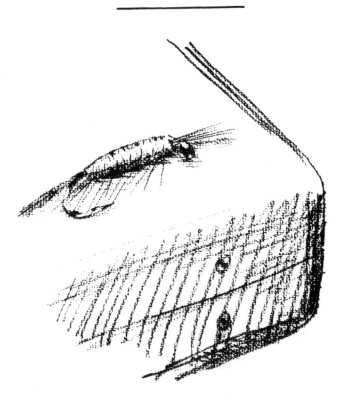

Hook: No. 10-12
Tying thread: Olive or tan Monocord
Body: Golden olive rayon floss
Tail, legs and antennae: Ginger saddle hackle (all one feather)
Rib: Fine gold wire or tinsel

THERE ARE SCADS OF SCUD IMITATIONS, as almost any fly-pattern book will tell you. So why would anyone want to go to all the trouble of creating another one?

The answer, in my case, is that I didn't think any of the existing patterns could do the job. I cut my fly-fishing teeth on the Kamloops trout of British Columbia and a good scud imitation is essential for success in that fishery. Before and after the great spring insect hatches, freshwater scuds—gammarids—are mainstays of the trout's diet, and abundant scud populations are a primary reason why Kamloops trout grow so rapidly and fight with such remarkable vigor.

When I began fishing seriously for Kamloops trout, the standard local scud pattern was a simple dressing with an olive chenille body, palmered brown hackle and a deerhair overlay similar to that used in the Salmon Candy. It was easy to tie and caught an occasional fish when I tried it, but it never worked with the consistency I thought it should.

The reasons were obvious. The olive chenille was a poor match for the semi-translucent quality of the real thing, which was also much lighter in color. The palmered hackle also was a poor imitation of the legs of the natural; it stuck out stiffly at right angles to the body of the fly. The deerhair overlay also added unnecessary buoyancy that made the pattern float toward the surface between retrieves, something a real scud would never do. Other patterns were even farther off the mark in appearance and performance, so I decided to try to come up with something better.

The main problem was the hackle. Even the softest saddle hackle appeared stiff and lifeless in the water when tied palmer fashion over the body of the fly. Some other approach was necessary and the only one I could think of was to align the hackle parallel to the body. With that idea in mind, I tried stripping one side of a ginger saddle hackle feather and placing it under the fly's body, along the belly, so the fibers on the unstripped side of the feather hung down beneath the fly. The result looked far more realistic than palmered hackle.

But it also posed the problem of how to secure the hackle to the body. I had chosen fine gold tinsel or wire for ribbing to give the body a natural-looking segmented appearance, and the ribbing material offered a way to kill two birds with one stone: It also could be used to bind the hackle feather to the fly. When I tried that, the results looked good.

While working on the hackle problem I also had been searching for a better body material. Translucent synthetic materials weren't available then, so I tried chenille, floss, dyed seal's fur, raffia and other materials in a wide range of colors, finally deciding rayon floss held the most promise. It was easier and quicker to apply than seal's fur and a lot less expensive in both financial and environmental terms, and after absorbing water it exhibited some of the semi-translucent quality I was seeking.

The next step was to find the right color. This took a long time because there's a big difference between the way rayon floss looks when it's dry and the way it looks in the water. Floss darkens and changes color when it becomes wet and you can't tell exactly what color fly you have until you've fished it under water for a while. The color I finally selected looked more gold than olive when the floss was dry, but when it was wet the color darkened to a shade I thought closely imitated the pale yellow-olive color of most real gammarids.

When all these ingredients were combined, the result was a pattern that, to me, looked and acted amazingly like the real thing.

THE NEW FLY RECEIVED ITS FIRST TEST in British Columbia's Hihium Lake. It was September, the week after Labor Day, and most other anglers had gone home to put the kids back in school, so I had the lake mostly to myself.

Except for an occasional fall of flying ants and a few chironomids, not much goes on in the way of insect hatches at Hihium in early September, but it's prime time for scuds. Trout often move in over the lake's shallow shoals during the day to root around for scuds in rocky crevices or underwater weeds, and this offered an excellent opportunity to try the new imitation.

I tried, tested and tweaked several versions of the new pattern until I found one that demonstrated consistent effectiveness, taking nearly one hundred trout during four days of fishing. Stomach samples revealed the trout had been feeding on scuds of a size and shape that closely matched the new imitation, prompting me to write in my diary that the new pattern "is well proven now, I think, and will become a regular part of my fly assortment."

It still needed a name, however, and I decided to call it the Golden Shrimp, bowing to the prevailing nomenclature in the fly-pattern books: Scud patterns were always called shrimps, even if scuds aren't true shrimps. In retrospect I should have called it something else. Now the Golden Shrimp itself has appeared in several pattern books and it's too late to change the name.

By any name, however, the Golden Shrimp remains my pattern of choice whenever scuds are present and trout are feeding on them. It is usually most effective during the middle of the day, retrieved slowly in two or three feet of water, or at slightly greater depths if the sun is full upon the water. Sometimes it's also successful as an evening fly, though it seems a little less consistent then.

The dressing has not changed since that week of testing at Hihium Lake many years ago. The Golden Shrimp remains one of very few patterns I still tie exactly the same now as I did when it was first conceived.

THE LIST OF MATERIALS NEEDED TO TIE THE GOLDEN SHRIMP is only half the story; the rest is in how those materials are applied. Here, briefly, is the sequence:

Choose a ginger saddle hackle feather with center fibers about three-eighths of an inch long on each side of the quill. Strip the fibers from the midsection of the feather on one side, leaving them intact on the other. The butt of the hackle and about half an inch of the hackle tip also should be left intact (not trimmed on either side); some of the butt fibers will serve as antennae and the hackle tip will serve as the tail of the fly. Thus, only the middle portion of the quill should be stripped, and only one side of that.

After stripping, secure the hackle feather to the bend of the hook so the tip extends backward and down to form the tail. The feather should be tied to the hook just at the point where the trimmed section begins; take care not to bind the fibers of the untrimmed portion under the tying thread.

After securing the feather, push it out of the way temporarily to make room for the ribbing and body materials. Tie in a length of fine gold tinsel or wire for the ribbing and four strands of golden olive rayon floss for the body. These should be secured just forward of the spot where the feather was bound to the hook.

Wind the floss forward to a point just behind the eye of the hook and continue winding back and forth until you have built up a full, cigar-shaped body. Tie off the floss behind the eye of the hook and trim away any excess.

Then take the hackle feather and place it along the belly of the fly stripped-side up and tight against the body so the fibers on the unstripped side are free to hang down and serve as the fly's legs. Using several turns of tying thread, secure the butt end of the hackle feather just behind the eye.

Now comes the tough part: Begin winding the fine gold wire or tinsel over the body and the hackle, using a dubbing needle to separate individual hackle fibers to keep them from being bound under the wire. This requires a sharp eye and the ultimate in patience. Be sure to keep tension on the wire so it binds the hackle feather tightly to the body. When the fly is fully ribbed, tie off the wire just behind the eye and trim the excess.

(I tried using two hackle feathers on early prototypes of the Golden Shrimp to simulate the double row of legs on the body of a real scud, but that required so much time separating fibers with a dubbing needle that I finally decided the trout probably wouldn't be counting the number of legs anyway; one hackle would have to be enough.)

The final step is to double over the butt section of the hackle feather so that some long fibers near the butt extend forward over the eye of the hook. Wrap the doubled-over feather with tying thread to keep these hackle fibers in place to serve as the antennae of the fly. Trim away any excess hackle, finish the head, apply a liberal coat of lacquer and the fly is finished.

THE PROCESS OF SEPARATING INDIVIDUAL HACKLE FIBERS with a dubbing needle takes a long time, especially for a slow fly tyer like me.

Usually it takes at least twenty minutes to finish a single Golden Shrimp, and the only reason I remain willing to invest that much time is because the results always have been worth it.

After its successful trial at Hihium, I tried the Golden Shrimp in other British Columbia waters. The first time I fished the new pattern at Peterhope Lake I caught more than a dozen Kamloops trout during a swirling snowstorm. Its inaugural use at Lundbom Lake produced eight heavy trout, all of which had been feeding heavily on scuds. Lundbom has—or used to have—a tremendous scud population, and I wrote in my diary that "I have always thought that if this fly were really effective it would work in this lake—and today's results remove any lingering doubts about its effectiveness."

On a return trip to Lundbom I had a take on my very first cast with a Golden Shrimp. I set the hook and watched in awe as a great trout vaulted out of the water. After a spirited ten-minute battle I netted a Kamloops trout that weighed six and one-half pounds on my pocket scale.

It was a great way to start a fishing day, but after that nothing happened for a long while. I could see dark, spawn-bound fish rising steadily in a nearby shallow bay, but paid them no heed until a fly fisherman casting from shore hooked a bright fish. The fish headed for the middle of the lake and never stopped; it took all his line and all his backing and finally broke the backing knot against a bare spool. Bereft of both line and backing, the angler was forced to stop fishing.

Thinking that where there had been one bright fish there might be others, I moved into the bay and began covering the same water the unlucky angler had been fishing. I hooked a very large bright fish almost immediately but lost it when the fly came away. This was followed by a dark fish of about five pounds that I released. Next came a bright, beautiful four-pound trout, gorged to the gills with olive scuds. After that I hooked two more fish, both large and bright, but both escaped after a long struggle. The activity finally halted when the sun slipped over the horizon, but in several hours of fishing I had hooked six fish, all large, and the fishing never had seemed slow. All six fish had taken a Golden Shrimp.

The pattern also proved itself in Corbett, Salmon, Roche and Gypsum Lakes and many waters around Little Fort north of Kamloops. Of the latter, I especially remember a small walk-in lake in the Aurora chain. It was a bitterly cold late-autumn day and a gusting wind had driven me to take shelter in a small bay, where the water was calm enough that I could see trout cruising over the pale marl bottom of the lake. The trout obviously were feeding on scuds, and if Kamloops trout could "light up" the way some saltwater fish do, these trout would have been positively glowing.

Using a Golden Shrimp on a sinking line, I cast ahead of one of the cruisers, let the fly sink to the bottom, waited for the trout to get close and then gave the fly a little twitch. The sudden movement kicked up a little cloud of silt; the trout saw it, bolted forward and seized the fly with a strike that felt like I'd hooked a sunken engine block. The same sequence was repeated time after time; it was totally absorbing fishing, one of few times I have been able to see fish approach and take a sunken fly.

The Golden Shrimp had proved its worth in the Kamloops trout lakes, but I was curious to see if it would work in other venues. Most waters close to my home have no scud populations, but there are a couple of very significant exceptions: Scuds are abundant in Puget

Sound and Hood Canal. These saltwater gammarids are found in large numbers among the thick mats of saltwort or pickleweed that grow along the beaches, and closely resemble their freshwater counterparts in size and color. I had found them often in the stomachs of sea-run cutthroat, so I decided to see if sea-runs would take the Golden Shrimp.

The results were gratifying. The Golden Shrimp not only took many sea-runs but also the occasional coho salmon, striped sea perch or starry flounder. I now use the Golden Shrimp whenever I fish around mats of saltwort or pickleweed.

Many other scud patterns have appeared since I began tying the Golden Shrimp. Most utilize synthetic materials and are much quicker and easier to tie than the Golden Shrimp. I've tried them mainly for that reason and a few have found places in my fly boxes, but the Golden Shrimp still outfishes all the rest. That's why I remain willing to spend the extra time it takes to tie it.

Curved "shrimp hooks" had yet to appear on the market when I began tying the Golden Shrimp, but I quickly bought some when they did. It didn't take long to decide I didn't like them. Not only did their hooking qualities seem less certain than those of conventional straight-shanked hooks, but I thought they actually resulted in a less realistic-looking fly. The reason: Scuds swim with their bodies held straight; they assume the familiar curved "shrimp" shape only when at rest. Since trout normally feed on free-swimming scuds, it doesn't make a whole lot of sense to tie imitations on curved hooks. When I tried it, the results proved the point.

After a fair trial of the curved hooks, I went back to tying the Golden Shrimp on conventional hooks.

AT THE TIME I BEGAN WORKING ON THE PROTOTYPE of the Golden Shrimp, in the late 1960s and early 1970s, I was also flirting with the idea of buying a fishing camp.

The notion stemmed from a visit to Thuya Lakes Fishing Camp near the tiny community of Little Fort. Thuya was then accessible only by a road that was rough enough to break the engine mounts of a pickup truck (as it did to mine). Survivors of the trip eventually came to a rustic lodge surrounded by a cluster of cabins between a pair of small lakes, Thuya on one side and Island on the other. The camp also offered access to more than a dozen other waters, mostly on a hike-in basis, and Thuya was one of few places offering the chance of a near-wilderness fishing experience.

During the course of several trips to Thuya, my wife, Joan, and I became friends with the owners, Ross and Dot Beebe. We happened to be there at a time when urgent family business demanded their presence elsewhere, so they asked us to look after the camp while they were away. This was no small responsibility, for the season was extremely dry and the lodgepole forest around the camp was virtually crackling with fire danger. Several guests canceled reservations because of the fire danger, so it turned out that Joan and I ended up with the entire camp to ourselves.

I still remember the utter silence of the place. There was no telephone, no radio and no television. We were far from the nearest paved road, so there were no traffic sounds. We were also far from any established aerial route, so there were no sounds of airplanes. The thick pine woods were hushed; even the birds were still. It was, I think, the most perfect silence I have ever experienced, magical in some ways but a little eerie in others.

Those days we spent alone at Thuya planted the idea that we

should have our own fishing camp. I suppose most anglers have similar dreams at one time or another, probably because the thought of owning a fishing camp carries with it the attractive notion of having your own private water to fish. Usually the idea never gets much beyond the dream stage, but that wasn't the case with us. We were young then and all things seemed possible; we both loved the outdoors and the thought of living in it, and of course I was captivated by the concept of being able to fish every day in my own water.

We weren't so naive as to think it would be easy. We had spent enough time at Thuya and other fishing camps to understand that running one is very hard work. It also requires one to be a jack-of-all-trades—mechanic, carpenter, plumber, electrician, and all-around handyman—and I had neither the experience nor the talent for any of those things. But with the incurable optimism of youth I figured a little on-the-job training would compensate for those deficiencies.

The more we thought about it, the more we were tempted by the prospect, so we started scanning advertisements, looking for fishing camps being offered for sale. We found a couple, including one that had once been among the most famous fishing lodges in British Columbia.

When we went to look it was immediately obvious why the place was for sale: The camp and its fishing had both seen their best years. The large trout were all gone from the camp waters and the cabins bore the marks of hard use by a couple of generations of fishermen, not to mention countless generations of carpenter ants. The docks and smokehouses leaned precariously and the outboard motors, if they could be started at all, sprayed oil and belched thick clouds of exhaust. If this place had any future, we quickly decided it did not include us.

This experience, while somewhat disillusioning, did not deter us from our dream. It did make us more cautious, however, and we decided it would be prudent to talk with the owners of some successful camps—places that *weren't* for sale—to see what advice they could offer. When we did that we were amazed at the unanimity of what we heard. Virtually every fishing-camp owner told us the same thing: If you like to fish, don't buy a fishing camp, because you'll be too busy ever to fish again, and if you like to eat, don't buy a fishing camp, because you'll never make enough money to keep food on the table.

That sobering advice, and the emphatic manner in which it was delivered, was enough to cool our youthful ardor. We decided our future role in fishing camps would be limited to that of customers.

That was more than thirty years ago, and we've never had reason to regret the decision.

THOUGH I LONG AGO GAVE UP THE IDEA of owning a fishing camp, the thought of fishing private waters has never lost its appeal. Over the years I've been fortunate enough to receive invitations to fish several of them.

One was Walker Lake, a small water located on a mountaintop in north central Washington State. I don't know who owns it now, but at the time it was owned by a syndicate that included my friend Ralph Hart. Ralph had told me about the lake in several conversations that always seemed to end with him saying something like "we'll have to get you over there someday." But "someday" never seemed to come.

Then one day it finally did: Ralph phoned to propose a firm date, gave me directions and suggested I take a friend since nobody else would be there when I arrived. There was an old hunting lodge at the lake where we could stay, he said.

I invited John de Yonge to go with me and we made the long drive together from Seattle, arriving well after dark. The rambling, ghostly shape of the old hunting lodge loomed forbiddingly in the headlights of my truck; it reminded me of the spooky old hotel in the horror movie *The Shining*. The keys were where Ralph had said they would be, and the door swung open on creaking hinges to reveal a dark, cavernous interior. Using flashlights for illumination, we entered and found a second doorway that led into a great central hall with a vaulted ceiling that soared beyond the reach of our flashlight beams. A huge stone fireplace occupied the center of the great room and the dim light disclosed a second-floor balcony with many doors leading to other rooms.

It was silent and eerie in the old lodge and for some reason we began speaking in hushed tones, as if fearful of awakening slumbering spirits. Then John found a light switch, tried it, and the great hall was flooded with light, which immediately reduced its apparently limitless dimensions to something merely large. We started speaking in normal tones and resumed our tour of the place, finding other working light switches that chased away the mysteries of the lodge.

We also found a handwritten journal that other anglers had left, and thumbed through it eagerly in search of information about the fishing. Along with numerous catch records we came across several references to unexplained noises and other mysterious doings in the night. Those passages were a little unnerving; as we spread our sleeping bags, we wondered if we might receive some unexpected nocturnal company. But we slept soundly without being disturbed by so much as a single ghost, and early the next morning we headed out on the lake.

A thick cloud layer had settled almost to the surface, making it difficult to see across the lake's forty-acre width. The cloud was emitting a cold drizzle and the thermometer on the lodge veranda registered a chilly forty degrees. It remained stuck there all that day and all the next while rain continued to fall, sometimes increasing nearly to deluge proportions. We fished hard despite the miserable conditions and caught good numbers of rainbow trout to three pounds on a variety of different flies, but I went away feeling that we had never really figured out exactly what was going on in the lake, or what the trout were eating.

Conditions weren't much better—in fact they were a little worse—when I returned the following year after another invitation from Ralph. This time Dave Draheim was along and we were startled to find an inch of fresh snow on the ground when we got up the first morning. The temperature was thirty-four degrees and the lake was shrouded in dense fog. Fishing was brutal.

By afternoon the fog had lifted to disclose a larch thicket along the lake's northern shore, the trees gleaming in their yellow autumn dress. The air warmed all the way up to the mid-forties and the fishing warmed up along with it; I landed a fish, went to remove the fly and noticed the trout's mouth was full of squirming olive scuds. It was the first clue I'd had that the lake held scuds, although I should have guessed it did. I clipped off the fly I had been using, replaced it with a No. 12 Golden Shrimp, resumed fishing, and in the next couple of hours landed fifteen rainbows up to three and one-half pounds, all short, blocky, powerful fish.

The next morning was clear and frosty and the temperature had plunged to thirty degrees. A thin layer of ice had formed around the rim of the lake but we broke through it and went fishing anyway. The morning fishing was slow, as it had been the day before, and the afternoon brought a bothersome wind that made fishing difficult. Nevertheless, during brief periods of relative calm, the Golden Shrimp again proved its worth by seducing another fifteen trout. Four others broke off and escaped with the fly.

We spent four days at Walker Lake, enduring another skiff of snow and even colder temperatures. The fishing remained slow in the mornings, brisk in the afternoons. Most trout we caught weighed about three pounds; the largest an even four. It was a good example of the type of fishing for which private waters are noted. It also was a good example of the effectiveness of the Golden Shrimp; the Walker Lake trout took it as avidly as teenagers gobbling french fries.

Some people contend private waters offer an artificial fishing experience. Such waters, they argue, are fished so lightly the trout in them are naive, even gullible, and hence too easy to catch. The light fishing pressure also gives trout the opportunity to grow to large size, so private waters often provide fast fishing for large fish and plenty of them—and that's just not the way things are in the real world.

Perhaps. But if you think about it, private waters actually may be closer to the "real world" than hard-fished waters open to the public. Before North America became overpopulated with fishermen, lightly fished waters full of large, gullible trout were the rule rather than the exception—and this, presumably, is what nature intended. Now most of these waters are public fisheries with intense angling pressure for small, wary, highly educated trout.

So which type of water provides the artificial experience? The answer, I think, is debatable.

Not that it really matters. I spend nearly all my time fishing hard-pressed public waters, so it's nice to have the occasional opportunity to sample a lightly fished private pond or stream. Variety, after all, is the spice of life—especially for anglers.

THE LAST PLACE MY FATHER AND I FISHED TOGETHER WAS Glimpse Lake, British Columbia. We were there during a period of unseasonably cold, wet weather, and the fishing was very slow. On our last day we fished hard from morning to dark in a steady downpour without seeing a single fish rise or feeling a single strike.

Perhaps it was the memory of that poor fishing, or maybe because the place reminded me that my father passed away at far too young an age, but for whatever reason I avoided Glimpse Lake for many years after that. Then a friend who had bought a cabin on the lake invited me to join him there and try the fishing, and I decided it was finally time to put aside unpleasant memories and give Glimpse another try.

Of course nothing was the same. The road to the lake, primitive and rough the last time I had been over it, had been graded and widened to near-freeway standards. As I drove in, a flagman waved me down and asked me to wait quietly for a few minutes while a movie company finished filming a scene next to the road. That never would have happened in the old days!

Those changes should have prepared me for what I would find when I reached the lake, but they didn't. When my father and I had been there, the lake was surrounded by thick forest; a small fishing camp was the only sign of human habitation. The fishing camp and much of the forest had disappeared and the lake was ringed with summer homes and cabins; it looked almost as if a small town had risen on its shores.

I decided I liked it better the way it was before.

But I found my friend's cabin, unloaded my gear and we went fishing. I rowed to the north end of the lake, near the site of the old fishing camp, and began searching the shallow, weedy shoals for signs of life. It didn't take long to discover that the water was full of swimming scuds, a situation made to order for the Golden Shrimp. I fetched one from my fly box, tied it to a long leader attached to a sink-tip line, and began casting.

After a few casts I was fast to a bright, husky trout that cartwheeled over the surface, then sought refuge in the weeds. I turned it away, forced it into open water and fought it until it surrendered.

I twisted the Golden Shrimp free from the trout's jaw, then grasped the fish gently and began moving it back and forth in the water to revive it. At first it was limp and listless, but then I felt little pulses of strength start rippling down its sides.

Suddenly my mind flashed back to the memory of that last long fishless day my father and I had spent here. Maybe things would have been different if we'd had a couple of Golden Shrimps with us then.

The fish was ready and I let it go.

"This one's for you, Dad," I whispered as I watched it swim away.

7

BLUE UPRIGHT

(HATCHMATCHER OR HATCHMASTER VERSION)

Hook: No. 16 3X fine dry-fly hook

Tying thread: Black

Tail, body and wing: Reversed metallic green feather from neck of mature wild Chinese pheasant rooster, or mallard breast feather dyed very dark blue

Hackle: Natural black dry-fly hackle tied fore and aft of wing

IT WAS MY FIRST FISHING TRIP TO THE SPRING CREEKS around Sun Valley, Idaho, and I needed advice about where to go and what flies to use. A friendly clerk behind the counter at Dick Alf's fly shop answered my questions and helped me choose some flies from the large selection on display.

Most of the fly patterns were familiar, but then something different caught my eye. It was a mayfly pattern, a small Green Drake, and it was the most realistic imitation I had ever seen. It was also incredibly delicate, as ephemeral as . . . well, a real mayfly. It looked as if it were about to rise out of the box on the counter and fly away.

I picked it up and made note of its unusual construction: Except for the hackle, the entire fly—tail, body and wing—had been tied from a single feather. I recognized the feather as mallard breast; it had been dyed light green, then reversed to form a lifelike extended body, with two fibers left pointing rearward as a V-shaped tail. The part of the feather left over after construction of the body had been forced into an upright position and trimmed to form the wing. A few turns of badger hackle on either side of the wing completed the simple pattern.

I was entranced. I doubted I would need any Green Drake imitations for the local spring creeks, but I knew I wanted some samples of this pattern to serve as models—because it seemed to me that here was a method of fly construction with almost infinite possibilities.

So I bought several of the flies, put them in a little plastic box and took them home, without realizing I didn't even know the pattern's name. Later I found out it was called the Hatchmatcher, or sometimes Hatchmaster, and either name was fitting. I also learned it wasn't a specific pattern so much as a generic style of tying, one that could be adapted to imitate virtually any mayfly species. I never did learn who invented this style, but Dick Alf has been credited with popularizing it, to the extent that it has ever become popular.

He certainly popularized it for me. Using the flies I purchased from his shop as models, I spent much of the following winter tying Hatchmatcher-style mayfly patterns. At first I used dyed mallard breast feathers, the same as those in the samples I had bought, but then I began experimenting with other feathers, including goose flank, pheasant rump, even dyed saddle hackle. All worked, but mallard breast and goose flank were best; they were easier to manipulate and held their shapes better than any of the others.

A fine imitation of the March Brown took shape from a plain, undyed brown mallard flank feather plus a few turns of brown hackle. A mallard breast feather dyed pale yellow and a few twists of ginger hackle resulted in a fly that put the Light Cahill to shame. A gray goose flank feather teamed with natural black hackle produced a fine imitation of the *Callibaetis* dun, and a plain, undyed gray mallard breast feather paired with grizzly hackle yielded an excellent *Ephoron* pattern.

But I still needed a good imitation of the spinner stage of the *Callibaetis,* and after trying and rejecting several combinations I finally hit on one with a mallard breast feather dyed very dark blue for the tail, body and wing, plus a few turns of natural black hackle. When I tied it, I had no idea this pattern ultimately would bring me more fish than all my other Hatchmatchers combined; I knew only that it looked like a good imitation of the *Callibaetis* spinner, the mayfly many anglers call the Blue Upright.

THE HATCHMATCHER VERSION OF THE BLUE UPRIGHT is simple to tie but the tying instructions are complex. Perhaps the best place to start is with a brief description of the anatomy of a mallard breast feather.

Each feather has a quill, or stem, thick at the butt and tapering gradually to a fine point at the tip. Fibers stick out on either side of the quill at an angle pointing toward the tip. These fibers are packed together closely and each has microscopic barbs that engage similar barbs on neighboring fibers, almost in Velcro fashion. This locks them together; in the vernacular of fly tyers, the fibers are "married." To tie a Hatchmatcher pattern, the feather must be reversed so the fibers point in the opposite direction—that is, toward the butt of the quill rather than the tip.

The first step is to choose a feather appropriate to the size of the hook; this takes a little experience but usually becomes second nature after a few tries. Once a feather of the correct size has been selected, the fluff at its base should be trimmed away. Then the quill should be cut near the tip, leaving a V-shaped section of feather. Only the quill should be cut, leaving all the fibers intact on the section of feather that will be used to make the fly. The cut-off tip section may be discarded.

A dubbing needle is then used to separate a single fiber on each side of the tip of the remaining V-shaped section of feather so the fibers are no longer "married" to their neighbors. The two separated fibers should be left pointing toward the tip of the quill in their natural V-shaped orientation; they will become the split tail of the fly.

The remaining fibers of the trimmed feather section should then be taken between thumb and forefinger and stroked carefully toward the butt of the quill, in the opposite direction from their normal orientation. At first they will resist being made to point in this direction, but repeated stroking will overcome this natural resistance. Even when all fibers are finally pointing in the right direction, however, it is still necessary to keep them pinched tightly between the thumb and forefinger or they will soon return to their original posture.

Once the fibers are all going in the right direction—toward the butt of the quill—they can be squeezed together tightly to form what looks very much like the body of a mayfly adult, with the two V-shaped fibers at the tip providing a realistic tail. The compressed body should be placed about three-eighths of an inch behind the eye of a No. 16 hook and bound very tightly in place with tying thread; a tight, secure wrap is necessary to keep the fibers from slipping. For best results, the wrap should just cover the butt of the quill.

If everything has been done properly to this point, a fairly lengthy section of the feather should be left sticking out in front of the wrap, extending beyond the eye of the hook. Grasp this section between thumb and forefinger and force it into an upright position to serve as the wing; a couple of turns of tying thread around the base will help keep it in position, as will a couple of turns fore and aft of the wing.

Once the feather is secure in the upright position, it should be trimmed into the shape of a mayfly wing, with the height proportionate to the length of the body.

The final step is to select a hackle feather and tie it in just forward of the wing; only the very best dry-fly hackle should be used. The hackle should be wound figure-eight fashion fore and aft of the wing; this will provide additional reinforcement to hold the wing in place. At least two turns of hackle should be taken on each side of the wing. When this is done, trim away any remaining excess hackle, finish and lacquer the head, and the fly is ready for fishing.

This is all much less complicated than it sounds, and once you get the hang of it you can tie the pattern in less time than it takes to read the explanation.

THE FIRST HATCHMATCHER PATTERNS I TIED LOOKED awfully good sitting in the palm of my hand, but I had yet to find out what the trout thought of them. I decided to test them on an isolated pond I knew had a spring hatch of March Browns.

The hatch came up about midafternoon and trout started dimpling soon after the first duns appeared on the surface. I captured one of the flies and compared it to the pattern I had fashioned from brown mallard breast and brown hackle; the artificial looked like a good match. So I tied it on, worked out line and covered a nearby rise.

The fly settled on the surface and cocked nicely in the upright position—something my dry flies don't always do. It also floated well, projecting a realistic silhouette well above the water. A rainbow trout apparently thought so, too, rising to take the fly confidently. I set the hook, played the fish and landed it, then removed the delicate fly. I expected to find it crushed beyond re-use, but to my surprise it popped back into shape and looked as good as new. I resumed casting, covered another rise and hooked a second trout. By the time I landed that one, the brief hatch had petered out and dry-fly fishing was over for the day. But it was an auspicious beginning for the Hatchmatcher.

A few weeks later I was driving along a stretch of the Ohanepecosh River in Mount Rainier National Park. The river looked so fetching I couldn't resist the impulse to stop and fish it. The Ohanepecosh derives its name from an exclamatory Indian word that translates roughly as "Oh, look!" and the river is definitely worth looking at. A happy, noisy little stream, it spills around rocks and ledges in the perpetual shadow of a great primeval forest, a river full of pocket water made to order for a light fly rod and a tiny dry fly. The trout inhabiting its cold, clear currents are like bright little jewels, gleaming with the colors of diamonds, rubies, emeralds and sapphires.

I could see a few tiny gray mayflies on the rumpled surface of the river, so I tied on a Hatchmatcher pattern and began making short, quick casts into pockets where I thought trout would hold. The fly set up nicely and floated well, even in the swift currents of the Ohanepecosh. I didn't fish long—the water was so cold it numbed my legs—just long enough to take two brilliantly colored cutthroat and a single sparkling rainbow on the Hatchmatcher pattern.

Later that summer the same fly seduced several fat, feisty brook trout during an afternoon hatch on an alpine lake in the high Cascades. That turned out to be my last dry-fly fishing of the year, but I was encouraged by the success of the new pattern.

I still had yet to test the Blue Upright version, however. Early next spring I got a chance on little Squalicum Lake, a pastoral body of water near my home town of Bellingham. I was with Lew Lund, a state fisheries biologist and old friend, and Dick Thompson, another old friend and inventor of the TDC pattern described earlier. Our purpose was to sample the lake to determine if fly-fishing-only regulations would be an appropriate form of future management. To do that we needed to get a handle on the numbers and average size of trout in the lake and take stomach samples to get some idea of the variety and abundance of food available.

Catching fish in seines would have been the most efficient way to do this, but it would be a lot more fun to go fishing. We rationalized this choice by convincing ourselves the only way to establish the lake's potential for fly fishing was to fish it.

So we did. Right away I noticed a few *Callibaetis* spinners on the water, some still laying eggs, others already spent and dying. Occasional rises indicated the cutthroat had noticed them, too. I tied on one of the Blue Uprights I had made from a dyed dark-blue mallard breast feather and a natural black hackle, and started covering rises. In the next hour I landed five cutthroat.

Stomach samples from these and other fish showed the trout were eclectic feeders—they had a little bit of everything in their stomachs, including *Callibaetis* spinners. The lake appeared capable of producing trout of reasonable size if they could be protected from angling predation long enough to grow; one way to assure that was to place the lake under fly-fishing-only regulations with a reduced bag limit. That was our recommendation and the State Game Commission approved it.

More than three decades later, Squalicum Lake is still under the same form of management and has become a popular and productive spot for fly fishers from my old home town. For me it also enjoys the distinction of being the first place I saw a trout rise to one of my Blue Uprights.

MAYFLIES OF THE GENUS *CALLIBAETIS* are spread widely over the waters of the West. Mainly a stillwater insect, the *Callibaetis* is found in lakes on both sides of the Cascade Range from northern California to British Columbia. It is the mayfly most often encountered by anglers over that vast area, and they call it by several different names in addition to Blue Upright.

The dun, or first adult stage of the *Callibaetis*, is much different in appearance from the spinner. Newly hatched duns are uniformly gray in color and larger than the spinners; those lucky enough to survive the predation of rising trout and swooping swallows fly to shore and seek shelter in lakeside vegetation, where they undergo a final molt and the *Callibaetis* spinner emerges.

The spinner has a segmented body of very dark blue, almost black, with thin gold bands dividing the segments; this dark blue color sometimes fades to creamish-brown on the belly of the fly. The wings of the spinner are transparent except for dark mottling along their leading edges; this mottling is responsible for another of the fly's popular names, the Speckle-Winged Spinner. But when viewed from a distance, either in the air or on the water, the spinner looks blue, accounting for the name Blue Upright.

The spinner is the final stage of the mayfly's life. After molting into the spinner stage, adult flies copulate in mid-air and the females return to lakeside foliage to wait until their fertilized eggs are ready for laying. Then they fly over the lake and dip repeatedly to the surface, depositing eggs each time until all their eggs are gone.

These flights usually begin about noon on late spring or early summer days and peak a couple of hours later. When the females have exhausted their eggs and their energy, they fall to the surface and struggle to rise again but lack strength to do so. For a while they float on the surface with wings held erect, quintessential Blue Uprights, but exhaustion finally makes it impossible for them to hold their wings upright any longer. The wings droop until at last they touch the surface; the insect, now completely spent, lies spread-eagled and helpless. During each of these stages—from egg-laying flight to final exhaustion—the spinners are vulnerable to feeding trout.

Most Western lakes have at least small hatches of *Callibaetis*, but some have emergences of extraordinary proportions. One of the most remarkable is on Oregon's Hosmer Lake, where I have enjoyed dry-fly fishing that sometimes can only be described as sublime.

Hosmer, of course, is where I learned to fish Lloyd Frese's Salmon Candy pattern, a wonderfully effective fly when caddisflies are hatching. But caddisflies don't hatch every day on Hosmer Lake; sometimes they don't hatch for days on end. By contrast, seldom a spring day passes without a thick swarm of *Callibaetis* spinners in the afternoon. Sometimes both caddisflies and *Callibaetis* spinners are on the water simultaneously, leaving anglers wondering which to imitate—but that's a pleasant problem, for it's always better to suffer an embarrassment of riches than face poverty.

The first day I fished Hosmer I saw plenty of spinners but didn't try to imitate them because the fish were obviously feeding on caddisflies. In fact, it was a couple of years before I fully understood the importance of Hosmer's spinner flights. That happened during a trip when I had fished a Salmon Candy without success for two days while waiting in vain for a caddisfly hatch. I could see salmon taking something from the surface the whole time, and *Callibaetis* spinners were the only things I could see that they might be taking. So on the third day I decided to try a Blue Upright.

A strong breeze was blowing, as it often does at Hosmer, and each gust dislodged fresh coveys of *Callibaetis* spinners from the rushes growing around the shoreline. The wind sent many of these flies tumbling to the surface, and I caught a glimpse of a large fish working its way along the shore, tilting upward now and then to inhale a spinner.

I cast ahead of the fish and watched as it approached. It rose gently and took the Blue Upright. I set the hook and the fish continued upward, bursting far out of the water in a great curving leap. It fell back with a splash, then ran hotly toward the shoreline reeds where I was afraid it would break off. Putting dangerous pressure on the light leader, I managed to turn the fish short of the threatening jungle. It leaped a second time, then we traded line for what seemed a long while until the salmon finally broached on the surface.

It weighed six pounds in the net. The No. 16 hook of the Blue Upright was embedded in its tongue, forever resolving any doubts I might have had that such a big fish would rise to such a small fly.

I landed three more large salmon that day, all on the same Blue Upright. Their many high-speed runs blunted the pawl in my Hardy LRH reel, reducing its shrill sound to a hoarse whisper.

The next day the spinners were back, although not in such large numbers; rises were fewer as a result. Nevertheless, the Blue Upright tempted a heavy fish that ran far into the backing before it straightened the No. 16 fine-wire hook and escaped. Later I hooked another that made three trips into the backing, further silencing the Hardy LRH. That fish registered five and one-half pounds on my pocket scale.

After that, the Blue Upright joined the Salmon Candy to form the one-two punch in my Hosmer Lake fly selection, and my diary is filled with accounts of many days when the Upright took twenty or thirty fish or more. Further experience taught me that on rare occasions when Hosmer Lake is calm, the salmon sometimes feed very selectively on spent-wing spinners, ignoring those whose wings are still upright. So I began tying Blue Uprights that weren't upright, dividing the single wing into two and tying the fly so that each wing stuck out horizontally at right angles to the body. The pattern worked when I tried it; I later found it worked even better if tied without hackle.

I also found success with the Blue Upright on other waters—Oregon's Davis Lake, Washington's Chopaka Lake, many British Columbia lakes. I even used it in New Zealand, where the Blue Upright captured a brace of heavy trout in the mighty Clutha River below its outlet from Lake Wanaka.

I HAVE ALWAYS BEEN PUZZLED why more people haven't adopted the Hatchmatcher or Hatchmaster style of tying. Considering the lengths to which some tyers go to construct mayfly imitations—elaborate detached bodies, exotic dubbing combinations, parachute hackles, burnt wings, etc.—the Hatchmatcher is simplicity itself. Not only that, but it produces a far more realistic imitation than any I have seen created by other methods.

Using different feathers or different color combinations, the Hatchmatcher style can be adapted to match any mayfly species. I carry six different versions in my portable "filing cabinet" of flies and know I can quickly construct others if I need them.

The Hatchmatcher also is extraordinarily durable. It looks so delicate you wouldn't think it could survive a single fish, but its delicacy is the very reason for its durability—there is virtually nothing a trout can sink its teeth into. If a hooked trout bends the wing or flattens the hackle, each will quickly return to shape as soon as the fly is removed from the fish. I have caught as many as twenty trout on the same Hatchmatcher without having to replace it.

It's not as if the Hatchmatcher style of tying were a secret; it has been described in several books. Maybe its false appearance of fragility is one reason it isn't more popular, or maybe the reverse-feather technique appears more intimidating than it really is (if I can do it, any tyer can!). Whatever the reason, I know of only a few others who tie and fish the Hatchmatcher regularly—but I think they would agree it's the best of all mayfly imitations.

SEVERAL SEASONS OF TYING AND FISHING BLUE UPRIGHTS finally exhausted my supply of dyed dark blue mallard breast feathers, but rather than go through the messy, time-consuming trouble of dying another lot, I decided to search for a substitute.

At first I found nothing suitable, but then one day I had the idea of trying to reverse a dark, metallic-green feather from the neck of a Chinese pheasant rooster, just to see what would happen. To my surprise, I found the feather lost its metallic green luster when reversed and became dark blue-gray in color, very close to the shade I was trying to match. Not only that, but it had a brown quill, similar to the color found on the belly of natural *Callibaetis* spinners.

The pheasant feather was a little harder to work with than mallard breast, but once reversed it seemed to hold its shape even better. And when I tested it on the Atlantic salmon in Hosmer Lake, the pheasant pattern proved at least the equal of the old mallard breast imitation.

Chinese pheasant rooster neck feathers were common and easy to get when I began using them. Many fly shops sold pheasant skins with the neck feathers still attached, and I had several bird-hunting friends who also brought me feathers.

But pheasant hunting has changed greatly in recent years. So much habitat has been lost that wild birds are now far less common than they used to be. These days, hunters are often forced to rely on farm-raised birds, released for sporting purposes like hatchery trout. For some reason—probably dietary deficiencies—these farm-raised birds seem unable to grow usable neck feathers.

Not surprisingly, the disappearance of wild Chinese pheasant from the fields also has meant the disappearance of their skins from the shelves of fly shops. Since the sparse, ragged neck feathers of farm-raised birds are useless for tying, they are almost always trimmed off before the skins of farm-raised birds are placed on sale.

I wasn't aware of any of this until I used up my supply of neck feathers and went looking for more. It was an unpleasant surprise to discover they were simply no longer available, either commercially or from any of my bird-hunting friends. If I wanted to tie more Blue Uprights—and I did—it looked as if I would have to go back to using dyed mallard breast.

But I refused to give up. Each time I visited a new fly shop I would check to see if it had any wild pheasant skins with neck feathers still attached. If none were on display, I would ask if there were any in the back room.

The answer always was no—until one day I walked into a new shop in the Olympic Peninsula town of Port Angeles. The young proprietor was friendly and we struck up a conversation while I examined the materials he had on display. He asked if there was something in particular I was looking for and I told him my sad story about Chinese pheasant rooster neck feathers.

He grinned. "I've got a whole bunch of them in the back room," he said. "I still get a few wild-bird skins with neck feathers, but I always cut them off because I didn't know anybody used them for anything. I've been saving them up and wondering what to do with them."

He went into the back room and came out with a large plastic bag filled with some of the best-looking Chinese rooster neck feathers I'd seen in a long time. Delighted, I dumped the contents on the shop counter and went through it, setting aside the very best feathers until I had a pile large enough to last the rest of my life.

"How much?" I asked.

"Oh, how about five bucks for the lot?"

It was a deal, one of the best purchases of fly-tying materials I've ever made.

EVEN AFTER SPLITTING THE FEATHERS WITH MY SON, I still probably have enough to last the rest of my fly-tying life. But the Blue Upright has another ingredient as important as the feather used for the tail, body and wing—and that, of course, is the hackle.

The hackle situation is the opposite from that of neck feathers. The advent of "genetically engineered" roosters has made it possible to acquire dry-fly hackle of superior or excellent quality almost anywhere, provided you can afford it. That wasn't always true; when I started tying Hatchmatcher-style flies, most tyers relied on necks from Indian or Philippine gamecocks. These varied widely in quality, and sometimes necks that were advertised as suitable for dry flies turned out to be otherwise, especially if ordered sight-unseen from a mail-order supplier.

In those days everyone had his eye out for good hackle. That continuing quest led to one of the strangest episodes in the history of the Washington Fly Fishing Club.

It began when sheriff's deputies, acting on an anonymous tip, raided an illegal cockfight at an abandoned mink farm in a rural area south of Seattle. The deputies handed out citations to the cockfight sponsors and seized fifty-four live gamecocks and three dead losers to use for evidence in court. The live birds were held in captivity; the dead ones went into the freezer.

When the case went to trial, an attorney representing the birds' owners told the judge their owners wanted them back. The prosecutor argued the gamecocks met the state's definition of illegal gambling equipment and shouldn't be returned. The judge sided with the prosecutor, whereupon county authorities ordered the birds destroyed.

Sixteen roosters already had died in captivity; the thirty-eight survivors were put to death by lethal injection. The county then offered the carcasses for sale to the highest public bidder. Ever alert to the possibilities of obtaining some premium dry-fly hackle, officers of the Washington Fly Fishing Club decided to submit a bid of $1 per rooster.

It turned out that was the only bid received, so the club ended up the proud owner of thirty-eight dead gamecocks. Four were in such bad shape they were thrown into the garbage. The rest were separated from their feathers by club members at a unique "skinning party," during which copious amounts of Scotch whiskey were consumed.

Despite having been skinned by club members under the influence of single-malt whiskey, the gamecock necks contained some of the prettiest dry-fly hackle you ever saw. They were auctioned at a club meeting and many fly tyers went home toting plastic bags full of hackle. The auction proceeds were used to send deserving kids to summer camp.

Some of those hackles ended up on Blue Uprights. Who says the justice system doesn't work?

THERE IS EVIDENCE, MOSTLY ANECDOTAL BUT STILL PERSUASIVE, that *Callibaetis* hatches have declined in recent years in waters all along the West Coast, from California to Canada.

The hatches that still occur also now appear to come earlier than ever, peaking two or three weeks before they once did. This is especially true in high-elevation lakes, where the ice cover that used to remain until late May is now often gone by the beginning of the month—which might explain why the hatches are earlier and smaller. Global warming is a likely culprit, but other factors also may be at work. Many waters that once supported enormous mayfly hatches have long been managed as put-and-take fisheries, routinely overstocked with voracious hatchery trout that over the years have made great inroads into mayfly populations. Oil slicks from outboard motors undoubtedly have contributed to declining insect populations in other waters, and silt kicked up by unthinking float-tube fishermen in shallow lakes has surely smothered the eggs of many aquatic insects.

Hosmer Lake has not been exempt from this. Its mayfly hatches are still more prolific than those of most other waters, but nowhere near as intense as they once were. Hosmer also faces many problems in addition to declining hatches. Some years ago the lake's population of sea-run Atlantic salmon was replaced by true landlocked salmon from Sebago Lake in Maine, and these fish have fallen far short of their predecessors in terms of sporting qualities. The landlocks do not live as long, grow as large, rise as willingly or fight as well as the sea-run fish, and their introduction has led to a decline in the fishing from extraordinary to merely ordinary.

Other problems are due to irresponsible management. For reasons that defy explanation, the state began stocking brook trout in

Hosmer Lake, which already had a small self-sustaining population of brook trout. As a result of the stocking, the brook trout population exploded; swarms of fry appeared in the shallows, gobbling up nearly all the food in sight. As numbers increased, average size decreased, and now the lake has many brook trout in the eight- to ten-inch size range. On my last trip I caught more brook trout than salmon for the first time ever. The exploding brook trout population also is surely one reason for the decline of the lake's *Callibaetis* hatches.

As this is written, there is a movement afoot in Oregon to end stocking of "exotic" (non-native) fish species. This would clearly be wise policy in many instances, but because salmon are unable to spawn successfully in Hosmer Lake, it would mean the end of the lake's unique, highly popular Atlantic salmon fishery. Brook trout, on the other hand, can and do spawn successfully at Hosmer, so in the absence of salmon they would have the entire lake to themselves—an ironic result, since brook trout also are an exotic species in Oregon.

For all these reasons, the future of the Hosmer Lake fishery appears highly uncertain.

Equally uncertain is the future of the scenic area around the lake, which is under increasing attack by corrupt Forest Service bureaucrats. The problem began with congressional approval of a so-called "fee demonstration" program requiring people using Forest Service campgrounds, including the two at Hosmer Lake, to pay for the privilege of occupying property they already own as American citizens. In authorizing this dubious, highly unpopular program, Congress apparently overlooked a statutory provision offering liability protection to owners of lands used for public recreation; the provision applies only if such use is free, so the protection was lost as soon as fees were charged.

This exposed the Forest Service to the threat of lawsuits from persons injured by falling trees or other campground accidents. The Forest Service, however, saw this as an opportunity rather than a problem: an opportunity to cut more trees. After all, if a campground has no trees, then campers can't be injured by falling timber.

The Bend-Ft. Rock District of the Deschutes National Forest, where Hosmer Lake is located, began holding timber sales in campgrounds. Campgrounds at Davis Lake, Crane Prairie, Big and Little Lava Lakes and other spots in the Oregon Cascades were logged, leaving once scenic, shaded spots with about as much outdoor ambience as a strip-mall parking lot. The loss of wildlife and wildlife habitat was enormous.

All this happened without protest, but when the Forest Service announced plans to log the campgrounds at Hosmer Lake it ran into opposition. A group of Hosmer Lake anglers and campers called the Friends of Hosmer filed multiple appeals opposing the logging plans.

The appeals slowed but did not stop the destructive forces at work. As bureaucrats wrangled, logging crews chipped away little by little at the campgrounds, cutting more so-called "hazardous" trees each year (by Forest Service definition, *any* tree in *any* national forest may be considered hazardous).

Finally, in the fall of 2001, the last appeal was decided. Despite unchallenged evidence that Forest Service officials had submitted false testimony and violated both federal law and regulations, the Friends of Hosmer appeal was denied. That was no surprise; under federal regulations, the Forest Service (or the Farce Service, as I now think of it) is allowed to sit in judgment of appeals against its own actions. Guess how most appeals turn out.

So everything at Hosmer is threatened: Its breathtakingly beautiful surroundings, its mayfly and caddis hatches, its unique population of Atlantic salmon. If you want to enjoy any of these, the best advice is to go there soon.

Maybe I'll see you there. I'll be the one fishing a Blue Upright.

8

CRAZY CHARLIE

(ORIGINAL PATTERN)

Hook: No. 4-8 stainless steel saltwater hook
Tying thread: White Monocord (or color to match body)
Eyes: 1/8-inch silver bead-chain eyes
Tail: Ten or twelve strands silver tinsel, short
Body: Clear translucent monofilament or similar material over underbody of silver tinsel
Throat: Two white saddle hackles, tips flared outward

IT'S PROBABLY AGAINST THE RULES OF FISHING BOOKS to start a chapter about a bonefish fly with the account of a steelhead fishing trip, but that's how the story of the Crazy Charlie begins for me.

It was early October and I was looking forward to my initial trip to Christmas Island in January. But first there was the fall steelhead run in the Wenatchee River to think about and I was anxious to get there and try my luck. So I left Seattle early one morning, drove through the flaming autumn foliage of Stevens Pass, struck the Wenatchee in Tumwater Canyon and followed it eastward to a favorite spot near the town of Cashmere. There I parked my truck and reached for the duffel bag that held my waders, vest and other fishing gear.

When I opened the bag, the first thing I saw was a strange fly box sitting on top of everything else. Wondering where it could have come from, I picked it up and opened it.

There were two trays inside the box, each with multiple compartments—and all the compartments were stuffed with bonefish flies.

Then I saw the note:

"Dad—for Christmas Island. Have a good day."

It was signed "Randy."

Randy, of course, is my son. He was sixteen at the time and busy in school, so he hadn't been able to come along on the trip to the Wenatchee. But I suddenly realized that all those hours I thought he'd been hard at work studying in his room, he'd been busy instead tying flies for me to take to Christmas Island.

The box held eight dozen flies. Two dozen were Crazy Charlies.

I don't remember if I caught any steelhead in the Wenatchee that day, but it didn't matter; it had been a good day from the moment I saw those flies and the note from my son. Not just a good day; one of the very best days ever.

WITHOUT DOUBT, THE CRAZY CHARLIE is the most famous bonefish fly in the world. That is remarkable status for a pattern that has been in existence only since 1976.

That was the year Bob Nauheim, a California fly-fishing travel entrepreneur, was fishing the North Bight of Andros Island in the Bahamas with Charlie Smith, a well-known bonefishing guide. As the story goes, they noticed bonefish feeding on some tiny, nearly transparent fish known as glass minnows. Nauheim never had seen this before and asked Charlie if it happened often; the guide confirmed that it did. So that evening, back in camp, Nauheim sat down at a vise and started work on an imitation of the glass minnow.

The result was tested the next day. It worked so well that Charlie said, "Dat fly's nasty," inspiring Nauheim to name the new pattern the Nasty Charlie. Later, Nauheim sent some of the flies to Leigh Perkins, Sr., of the Orvis Company, who was planning a trip to Christmas Island. The pattern worked just as well for Christmas Island bonefish as it had in the Bahamas, but Perkins forgot the first part of its name and ended up calling it the Crazy Charlie. That name stuck.

The rest, as they say, is history. The Crazy Charlie's popularity spread rapidly among bonefish anglers until it became *the* pattern to use for bonefish all over the world. It also inspired numerous variations, perhaps more than any other fly pattern, and eventually the Crazy Charlie became more a generic style of tying than a specific pattern. Nauheim's original intent—imitating a glass minnow—was almost forgotten; most anglers now tie and fish variations of the Crazy Charlie as shrimp imitations.

The most distinctive feature of the Crazy Charlie, and just about the only one that has remained unchanged since Nauheim tied the prototype, is a pair of bead-chain eyes tied on top of the hook just behind the eye. The weight and placement of these eyes make the hook ride upside down in the water, which was Nauheim's original intent; with the hook riding up, the fly is much less likely to hang up on coral or weed.

Construction of the pattern begins with selection of a stainless-steel saltwater hook of appropriate size. The size depends on the depth of the water to be fished; the Crazy Charlie is designed to be fished on the bottom in shallow water, but "shallow" is a relative term. If you expect to be fishing in as much as three feet of water, then a No. 4 hook will get the fly to the bottom faster than a smaller size. Conversely, if the water is a foot deep or less, or if you're fishing the shallow wave surge over a coral reef, a No. 8 hook will do; anything larger will mean lots of hang-ups. A No. 6 hook is a good compromise for situations between these two extremes.

Once the hook is selected, the next step is to attach the bead-chain eyes. These should be placed just far enough behind the hook eye—about three-sixteenths to a quarter of an inch, depending on hook size—to allow space for the wing. The bead-chain eyes should be secured very firmly with repeated figure-eight wraps; when complete, these should be coated with epoxy or fly-tying cement.

The next step is to tie the underbody, and the materials for this should be secured just behind the bead-chain eyes. The original Crazy Charlie had an underbody fashioned from multiple strands of silver tinsel; these were wound along the shank to a point just forward of the bend of the hook, and the ends of the strands were allowed to extend beyond the hook as a short tail. Silver (and gold) tinsel are still often used, but many Crazy Charlie variations now utilize other materials such as Flashabou, Holographic Flash, Krystal Flash, Flexi-Floss or other modern synthetics. As in the original pattern, these materials are wound along the hook shank to form the underbody, which should start fairly thick and taper to a thin diameter at the rear of the fly. Some variations include a tail while others do not.

The finished underbody is next covered by a wrap of transparent or translucent material. Bob Nauheim used clear monofilament for this purpose, but most tyers now use clear V-Rib, Larva Lace or similar materials. The purpose of this material is to give the fly an illusion of transparency, similar to that of a real glass minnow or shrimp.

Nauheim's pattern called for a pair of flared hackles tied in at the throat, but most tyers now use a single hair wing (calftail is a popular choice) tied sparsely, sometimes with a few strands of Krystal Flash mixed in to add extra sparkle to the fly.

My preference is to use different colors of Flexi-Floss, Krystal Flash or a combination of both for the underbody, although I also sometimes still use gold tinsel. The smallest size of clear V-Rib or Larva Lace is used to wrap the overbody. As for the wing, I have used calftail in both dyed and natural colors, but I think natural brown or reddish-brown foxtail works better; it is softer than calftail and gives better action in the water. As a final touch, I usually blacken the bead-chain eyes with an indelible marker; this makes the fly look more realistic to me, although I'm not sure the fish have noticed.

THAT BOX OF FLIES MY SON GAVE ME has since traveled many miles over the flats of Christmas Island in the Pacific and Turneffe Island in the Caribbean. All the patterns have been used at one time or another, but the Crazy Charlies were used most heavily. Of the two dozen originals only a few now remain, but those missing in action have been replaced by many more of my own.

My bonefish baptism occurred in one of the interior lagoons at Christmas Island. The day was cloudy with a strong breeze, which made it especially difficult to see fish, but with the help of polarized glasses and intense concentration I was able to glimpse occasional ghostlike shadows moving over the white coral sand. I kept casting toward these moving shadows and eventually a bonefish grabbed my fly and ran into the backing, convincing me that everything I had heard and read about these wonderful fish was true. When I landed the fish, I was amazed to see it weighed only about one and one-half pounds; how could such a small fish run with such strength? It had taken a Crazy Charlie variant with a body of pink floss covered by clear V-Rib.

After that, a long time passed without more fish, so I switched to another Crazy Charlie variant, this one with a flat gold tinsel body covered by clear V-Rib. It was just the ticket; I caught ten more bonefish that day and missed several others.

During the next few days I learned it was necessary to experiment at the start of each fishing session to see which fly the bonefish preferred that particular day. Some days it was pink and others it was gold. I tried other colors, but most were ignored. I never did learn the reason for this remarkable day-to-day change of preference.

That first trip taught me a lot of other things about fishing for bonefish. I learned to stay low so the fish couldn't see me and to make a careful presentation so that neither fly nor line would make a disturbance when it struck the water. I taught myself to wait patiently while the fly sank and begin stripping only when the fish approached it closely. If a fish turned and followed the fly, I learned to keep stripping until it got close, then stop to let the fly settle to the bottom. I found it was usually difficult to see the fish actually turn down and take the fly in its mouth, which made the timing of the strike mostly a matter of instinct—but when instinct kicked in, the strike had to be made quickly by simultaneously stripping line and sweeping the rod back in a horizontal arc.

Some of this I learned on my own and some of it I learned from guides, although on that first trip to Christmas Island it seemed most of the guides were still learning, too. Since then they have become much better at their trade, although under most circumstances I would still rather fish without a guide because I think it's more fun, and more satisfying, to find fish on your own.

I used a 7-weight rod and eight-pound test leader for bonefish on that first trip, so I was unprepared for the much larger and stronger trevally that also hang out at Christmas Island. One day, while wading an isolated flat in the main lagoon, I saw a large trevally coming toward me. I knew I didn't have the right equipment to handle such a big fish, but what angler could ever resist such an opportunity? When the trevally came within casting range I dropped my Crazy Charlie in front of it, not really expecting a fish of that size—it was probably twenty-five or thirty pounds—to be interested in such small prey. But the trevally jumped on the fly immediately and took me to the cleaners so fast I was lucky to get my fly line back. Later I had a similar experience with a somewhat smaller trevally, this one about ten pounds, which also escaped with one of my Crazy Charlies in its mouth.

I caught no trevally of any size on that trip, but I did catch many bonefish, the largest about six and one-half pounds, and left

Christmas Island with full faith and allegiance to the Crazy Charlie as a superior bonefish fly.

MY NEXT BONEFISHING EXPERIENCE WAS ON THE FLATS OF Turneffe Island, a huge coral atoll off the coast of Belize. Unlike Christmas Island, many flats at Turneffe Island are covered with turtlegrass and bordered by mangrove thickets. The turtlegrass makes it tough to see fish unless they are tailing, and the continually metastasizing mangrove roots seem made for the sole purpose of providing handy places for fleeing bonefish to break off a fly. This makes the Turneffe Island fishing environment somewhat more difficult than Christmas Island, but that merely adds to the challenge.

The first day at Turneffe Island I learned the Crazy Charlie worked just as well there as it had at Christmas Island. In this case, a small (size 8) version with an underbody of tan or beige Flexi-Floss and a couple strands of "root beer" Krystal Flash did the trick.

Such small flies were necessary because much of our fishing was in very shallow water over a reef. Even the size 8 patterns—the smallest I had—often hung up on the coral, and when my guide, Joe Faber, looked through my fly assortment and saw all had been tied with bead-chain eyes, he suggested next time I should tie at least a few with-out eyes. That way they wouldn't sink as quickly and hang up as often.

Before the day was out, he followed his own advice and used a knife to cut the bead-chain eyes off one of the flies Randy had tied. Using the virtually weightless fly, I hooked a large bonefish that ran far, took the fly around a coral head, and broke off.

During the week I spent at Turneffe Island I experimented with a number of different patterns from Randy's assortment and others I tied myself, including the Gotcha, Bonefish Special, Agent Orange and Crazy Charlies in several different colors. But it was the little Charlie with the tan and "root beer" Krystal Flash body that got the most attention from the fish.

THE BONEFISH HAS ONLY TWO FAULTS: It won't rise to a dry fly and it doesn't jump. In all other respects it is, I think, the perfect fish, and certainly one of the biggest reasons saltwater fly fishing is growing faster than any other branch of the sport. Considering the bonefish and all the other species and opportunities available in saltwater, it's no mystery why so many anglers are leaving crowded trout streams to try their luck in the ocean.

Yet not all is well in the world of saltwater fly fishing. Two spreading infections threaten the future health of the sport, possibly even its survival. One is an unfortunate preoccupation with the pursuit of records; the other is an even more unfortunate preoccupation with competitive fishing tournaments.

What's wrong with records? To begin with, fishing records are essentially meaningless; if they measure anything at all, it is opportunity, not skill. For a record to be meaningful, the "competition" must be open to everyone—and many anglers, if not most, refuse to take part because they aren't interested either in competition or records. That leaves a minority of anglers willing to compete, and among those few the odds are heavily in favor of those who can afford to spend the time and money necessary to travel to the best spots and hire the best guides. Not many people can do that, which narrows the "competitive field" even further, to a few well-heeled anglers. If one of these should happen to catch a "record" fish, it usually proves only that he or she had the economic means to do so, nothing more.

That some people are willing to do this is evidence of egos badly in need of gratification. Apparently they feel that having their names listed in a record book will give them fifteen minutes of fame—but it's a lot cheaper, and just as meaningful, to have your name listed in the local telephone book.

Not that ego doesn't play a role in fishing; few people would fish if they did not feel some sense of satisfaction or self-gratification from the experience. A little of that is healthy, both for the angler and the sport, but the single-minded, fanatical pursuit of records is not what fly fishing is all about; it compels people to fish for the wrong reasons.

The competition in saltwater fishing tournaments is no less illusory. Many anglers, if not most, have absolutely no desire to participate in tournaments, so once again the field is narrowed to a minority—which may very well not include the best fishermen. Many tournaments also have hefty entry fees, so again participation is limited to the relatively few anglers willing and able to afford it. Being able to pay the entry fee has nothing to do with one's angling qualifications, of course, and that makes the competition basically meaningless. Some tournaments try to get around this problem by teaming fishermen with expert guides, presumably on the theory that the latter will make up for the deficiencies of the former. Where's the competition in that?

Not all tournaments are limited to wealthy anglers, but even tournaments without extravagant entry fees have the potential to distort saltwater fly fishing the same way so-called "professional" tournaments have made a pitiful parody of the once great sport of bass fishing. The spectacle of dozens or hundreds of people racing around in high-speed boats in maniacal pursuit of the largest and/or the most of a species also directly undermines the work of countless anglers who have tried to foster an image of fly fishers as conservationists. Worse yet, it plays directly into the hands of extremist groups that seek to ban sport fishing altogether. It doesn't matter that most tournaments now require contestants to release all fish caught; the very nature of the competition unwittingly validates the arguments of organizations that view sport fishing as an unnecessary form of animal cruelty.

I'd be first to admit that some tournaments benefit worthy charities, but in fishing, as in every other endeavor, the end rarely justifies the means. There are plenty of other ways for charities to raise money.

I've also heard the argument that tournaments create opportunities for good fellowship among fishermen and stimulate innovation that benefits all anglers. But those "arguments" suggest there would be no good fellowship among anglers if it weren't for tournaments, and that's just plain bilgewater. Fellowship among anglers is natural and I suspect that the camaraderie among anglers not in competition with one another is likely to be more genuine than among those who are. As for stimulating innovation, natural market forces always have taken care of that, and always will.

Tournaments place fishermen in competition with one another for rewards in the form of prizes, trophies or other forms of recognition, and all these are contrary to the fundamental traditions of fly fishing; as with records, they make people fish for the wrong reasons. The only legitimate competition in fly fishing is that between the angler and the fish; the only legitimate reward is the thrill of deceiving a wild creature and winning the contest that follows. That should be enough for everyone.

IT WAS 3:30 IN THE MORNING AND I WAS ABOUT TO depart from Honolulu for another trip to Christmas Island. Trying to blink the sleep from my eyes, I hauled my gear down to the hotel lobby to wait for the airport shuttle. The lobby was dark and almost deserted at that hour; there was only one other person, a man seated in an overstuffed chair surrounded by mounds of gear, including several rod tubes—obviously another angler bound for Christmas Island.

With an accent that betrayed British origins, he introduced himself as Michael Wilkins. He explained that he was on a six-month holiday from his business of setting up international trade shows and was spending the time fishing his way around the world. He had just come from New Zealand and now he was ready to tackle Christmas Island. He was an interesting fellow and we hit it off immediately.

We rode to the airport together and found a crowd waiting for the weekly flight to Christmas Island. Some waiting passengers carried rod cases, a tip-off their purposes were the same as ours, but there was also a missionary family, some Christmas Island natives on their way home, and a few others whose origins or intentions were not clear. When we boarded, the Boeing 737 was almost full.

We took off and climbed to an altitude from which the Pacific was only a vague blue film beneath scattered white clouds. We had been flying about a half hour when I looked up from the book I was reading and noticed the sun was on the wrong side of the airplane; we were heading north, not south in the direction of Christmas Island. I was about to signal the flight attendant to ask what was going on when the captain came on the public-address system and announced the plane's electronic navigation system had failed. We were turning back to Honolulu.

The announcement was greeted with consternation. Many of us had expected to be fishing before the day was out; any delay would cut directly into our fishing time.

But there was nothing we could do about it, so we waited patiently in Honolulu while technicians replaced the defective navigation system and tested the new one to make sure it worked. Then we took off again and flew uneventfully to Christmas Island, arriving two and one-half hours behind schedule.

The old military airfield had changed little since my last trip nearly a decade earlier, but this time there was a much larger native contingent on hand to greet the arriving flight. I was also surprised to see a few beat-up cars available for rent—something nobody would have dreamed of ten years earlier. The customs inspectors also subjected us to a far more rigorous search than on my first trip, and it took a long time for them to go through everyone's baggage. More fishing time was being lost.

After clearing customs, we boarded an old school bus for the trip to the Captain Cook Hotel, the old British officers' quarters that would serve as our accommodations. It was an El Niño year and I had heard there had been heavy rainfall at Christmas Island, but I had no idea just how heavy it had been until the bus started driving through great pools of standing water. Water fountained through a hole in the bus floor and started running down the aisle, forcing passengers to raise their feet to keep from getting wet. Those who had stowed their gear on the floor found it soaked by the time we reached the Captain Cook.

All things considered, it wasn't an auspicious beginning for a fishing trip.

EVEN AFTER ALL THE DELAYS, we still managed to get in a couple of hours of fishing that first day, and the same little Crazy Charlie variation that had worked so well at Turneffe Island quickly won the approval of the Christmas Island bonefish. Wading the margins of an interior lagoon, I sighted several small pods of bonefish and many singles, all cruising in ankle-deep water over white coral sand. It had been a couple of years since my last bonefishing experience, so I was surprised I could see them so easily; apparently the long layoff hadn't affected my bonefishing "eye."

Four of the cruising bones took the little tan-bodied Crazy Charlie and responded in the usual manner by dashing across the flat, quickly pulling line well into the backing. They weren't big—the largest only about three pounds—but it was a joy to feel again their incredible electric strength, and a nice way to end a day that had begun so unpromisingly.

That night I was awakened by a deafening roar. For a frightening moment I had no idea where I was or what was happening; then I remembered I was in the Captain Cook Hotel and realized I was hearing the sound of torrential rain—rain with a capital R, tropical monsoon, deluge, Noah-and-the-Flood-type rain.

After a while the rain slackened, but twice more before morning I was awakened by similar roaring bursts. The rain was still pelting down when I went to breakfast, and water was standing in the courtyard and rushing in waterfalls from the gutters of the old British officers' quarters. The sky was an ugly pewter color.

At breakfast an Australian couple reported the thatched-palm roof of their bungalow had leaked during the night, soaking their beds and leaving an inch of water on the floor. The roof had just been replaced, but everybody knows it's hard to find reliable roofers these days and apparently that's as true on Christmas Island as it is everywhere else.

Through some sort of lottery I didn't quite understand, the chief guide announced that I would fish with Mike Wilkins and two other anglers, Renji Tow, an enthusiastic young fisherman from Massachusetts, and Boyd Poulsen, an Idaho pharmaceutical executive. We climbed into the back of a weather-beaten pickup truck with a U-joint that made dangerous clunking noises and drove to a place called Pass Flat on one of the interior lagoons.

Along the way we forded many more large pools of standing water. High tides had allowed small fish to reach some of these giant puddles and we watched fish flee in all directions as we drove through the pools—the only time I've ever seen a road with fish in its potholes. One long stretch was submerged under more than a foot of water and I had doubts the battered pickup would get through, but it did. Surveying the flooded landscape, I couldn't help thinking it wouldn't take much more rain to sink the whole island beneath the ocean.

The guides parked the truck along the roadside next to the flat and we waded out, skirting the edge of a sandy spit littered with the rusting wreckage of old British Army lorries left from American and British H-bomb tests—a chance for Mike Wilkins to see how some of his tax dollars had been spent. The flat stretched endlessly under a dark sky but the water was a sort of nauseous green color, filled with turbidity from the overnight storm. The pastel grays and greens along with the nearby military wreckage created a surrealistic scene, like something from an aquatic version of the movie *Mad Max*.

It was impossible to see fish under such conditions, so we started casting blindly. In quick succession I hooked a bonefish of about seven inches—my guide, Kauea, said it was "born yesterday"—a yellow snapper about the size of a silver dollar, and a small, colorful specimen Kauea identified as a goatfish, although it seemed far too pretty to warrant such a homely name.

Meanwhile, a great darkness was boiling up over the horizon, a greenish-black veil that reached all the way down to the wavetops, the Grim Reaper visage of an approaching storm. It struck within moments, stinging us with firehose bursts of rain and furious wind gusts that blew our backcasts into the water. The worst of the storm passed quickly, but steady rain fell in its wake. The fishing conditions, poor to begin with, had become impossible, so the guides suggested moving to a different place.

Dripping wet, we piled back into the pickup and drove over more flooded roads to a place called Navy Flat on the outskirts of a village where we could hear school bells ringing and children laughing. I thought the sounds added a certain charm to the spot.

Navy Flat was huge and looked great, although the light remained poor and there was a continuing spatter of rain on the surface. Unable to see fish, we began casting blindly again. My little Crazy Charlie brought no strikes—perhaps the fish couldn't see it very well under these conditions—so Kauea suggested I try a fly he had tied. It was a pattern constructed in the familiar generic style of the Crazy Charlie, with gold bead-chain eyes, a gold tinsel body and a wing of orange Krystal Flash. I tied it on and soon began hitting fish.

The first gave me one of the longest runs I've ever had, a wild series of lunging spurts that spooled a good one hundred and fifty yards of backing from the reel. After much arm-wearying reeling, I finally brought the fish close to hand. It circled us several times until Kauea reached for the leader, missed it, and the fly came away. He estimated the fish was twenty-eight inches and weighed eight and one-half pounds, which would have made it the largest bonefish I'd hooked up to that time.

It was soon followed by another good fish that ran nearly as far. This one I landed—a beautiful thick bonefish of about six pounds. Three smaller fish came after that, then two larger ones that each came unpinned after the first run. All took Kauea's fly, and at my request he promised to tie a couple more for me that night.

Eventually the fish stopped coming, both for me and the others, and it appeared they had abandoned the flat with the changing tide. We trekked back to the pickup, looking forward to a late lunch, but then discovered that while we had been fishing some of the kids from the nearby school had looted our cooler and stolen our sandwiches and beer. Navy Flat suddenly seemed a lot less charming than I'd thought, but we managed to console ourselves with the thought that the kids probably needed the sandwiches a lot more than we did. It was too bad about the beer, though.

We returned to the hotel wet, cold and hungry. We had waded and walked several miles, most of the time under heavy rain, and I felt as if I'd cast several miles worth of fly line. But the fish I'd caught made it all worthwhile.

THAT EVENING, MIKE WILKINS INVITED ME TO JOIN HIM FOR A DRINK and a cigar in what passes for a lounge at the Captain Cook Hotel. We were both enjoying our cigars and Victoria Bitters when two natives entered the lounge and ordered drinks at the bar, then came over and asked if they might join us. We quickly invited them to do so.

One was a tough-looking customer, a heavyset, mahogany-skinned, middle-aged man with a large, nasty-looking machete scar on his face. His friend was much younger, a handsome young man barely in his twenties. Each spoke a little heavily accented English, as most Christmas Island natives do, and despite his rough appearance the older man turned out to be polite and soft-spoken. I was surprised to learn he taught school on the island. Having established that, I turned to his young friend and asked what he did.

He grinned broadly and said: "I'm an asshole."

I bit down hard on the butt of my cigar to keep from laughing. Someone must have told him that was the correct response if anyone asked his occupation, and in his innocence of English he had fallen for the gag.

Further questioning revealed he was actually a ditch digger for a local water project. But his first answer left me chuckling privately; years later I still smile whenever I think of it.

NEXT MORNING WAS CLEAR AND SUNNY AND WE MOTORED ACROSS the main lagoon to a place called Y Site, an intricate labyrinth of tiny islets, lagoons, sandspits, channels and flats. I had been assigned a different guide, a pleasant young man named Bea, but before leaving the hotel I had found Kauea and paid him for the flies he had tied for me the night before.

We started fishing along the shore of an islet where countless tiny shells had washed up in terraced windrows on the beach and been bleached by the sun until they were as white as snow. Shells also littered the bottom where we waded, crunching underfoot like broken glass.

There was no wind—a rarity at Christmas Island—and it soon became blisteringly hot under the morning sun. Tiny fish darted in and out of coral ledges, a small spotted ray swam almost to our feet, and we spooked several blacktip reef sharks. Pufferfish lolled in the shallows, blowing themselves up like self-important politicians when they saw us coming. Spindly frigate birds, graceful terns and awkward red-footed boobies nested in low-lying scrub on the tiny islands and sandspits, and the infinite variety of shapes and colors of all these creatures reminded me forcefully there is no better place to appreciate the great diversity of life than a coral reef.

But we were after bonefish. The absence of wind had left the water's surface glassy and still so it was easy to see the wakes of bonefish cruising just under the surface—not just singles, but sometimes as many as fifty or sixty fish in a single school. Casting to one of these schools, I quickly hooked a fish that ran around the sandy point of a small island so I was on one side of the point while the fish was on the other and my line was actually running over dry land. Needless to say, that fish escaped, and so did most of the next few I hooked. Careless casts spooked several others. All the fish seemed exceptionally nervous in the still, shallow water under the bright sun, and by the time the skiff came to fetch us at 11 a.m., I'd hooked ten bonefish but landed only four.

After a short break for a sandwich and drink aboard the skiff, we resumed fishing. By then the horizon was again growing ominously dark with approaching squalls—huge, night-black, advancing storm cells that resembled the mushroom clouds of the H-bombs once exploded near here, and looked scarcely less threatening. The light dulled with their approach and the wind stirred, then began blowing briskly. I braced myself for another severe wetting, but the fast-traveling squalls miraculously passed us by.

Despite the deteriorating light we could still see the occasional fish, and during the next three hours I was into fish almost continually. Most were small, less than three pounds, but all fought with satisfying sizzle, and by day's end my score had reached twenty-eight bonefish. Most had taken Kauea's flies until I broke off one and a fish straightened the hook on the other; after that I switched to another Crazy Charlie variant of my own, one with a body of silver Krystal Flash covered by translucent V-Rib. It worked, too.

THE FISHING REMAINED GOOD FOR THE NEXT FEW DAYS and the weather cooperated most of the time. Feeling comfortable with my ability to see fish, I decided to go without a guide. Each day still required experimentation to see what color fly the bonefish preferred, and a chartreuse Crazy Charlie turned out to be the pattern of choice for the remainder of the week—the first time I could remember catching bonefish on a fly of that color. Fortunately, I had tied several Charlies with bodies of chartreuse Flexi-Floss and lime-green Krystal Flash, covered by the usual translucent V-Rib. Both had standard silver bead-chain eyes and sparse foxtail wings.

Later, looking through my notes from the trip, I realized the Crazy Charlie was the only fly I had fished. I'd used different colors and sizes, but every pattern was tied in the familiar Crazy Charlie style. Without even realizing it, I'd become an exclusive user of the Crazy Charlie for bonefish.

In retrospect that wasn't surprising, for a similar evolution has taken place in nearly every type of fishing I do, whether it's for trout, steelhead, sea-run cutthroat, Atlantic salmon, or whatever. In each case I started with a wide variety of fly patterns and gradually narrowed them to a few well-proven patterns—or, in the case of the bonefish, to only one.

But it's results that count, and the Crazy Charlie always seems to get them.

9

Judge Boldt

Hook: No. 6 or 8 low-water Atlantic salmon hook
Tying thread: Black
Tail: Brown deer body hair
Body: Black wool, thin
Wing: Brown deer body hair, tied upright
Hackle: Natural black dry-fly hackle, several turns fore and aft of wing

THE RISE OF A SUMMER STEELHEAD TO A FLOATING FLY is an unforgettable sight. It may be a prim, perfect, head-and-tail rise like that of a brown trout feeding delicately on mayflies in a chalk stream, remarkable only for the great size of the fish and the volume of water it displaces. More often it is a violent rush, a great lunge through the surface that sends water flying in all directions and lightning bolts stabbing down an angler's spine. There is no other sight quite like it in all of angling.

A dry fly capable of inducing such rises is something special. As such, it deserves a special name, something heroic or noble or inspiring. You would never expect anyone to name a steelhead dry-fly pattern after one of the most despised figures in Northwest angling history.

But that's what I did. And therein lies a tale.

UNITED STATES DISTRICT JUDGE GEORGE H. BOLDT *was* a hero to some people, but they were greatly outnumbered by the many who hated him. Fate chose the late judge to hear the landmark case of *United States v. Washington,* in which the federal government, acting as trustee for various Indian tribes, sought to enjoin the State of Washington from interfering with tribal fishing rights secured by federal treaties.

The case culminated seventy-five years of courtroom skirmishing and riverside confrontation over Indian access to steelhead and salmon runs. When Judge Boldt handed down his decision on February 12, 1974, he sided with the tribes on nearly every issue. He ruled the tribes had the right to catch half of all harvestable salmon and steelhead returning to "usual and accustomed" Indian fishing grounds, which included most steelhead rivers in Western

Washington. This right had been secured by treaty, Judge Boldt said; non-Indians had no such right. For them, fishing was merely a privilege.

The judge seized control of state fisheries management, ordering drastic cuts in both commercial and sport-fishing harvests. These reductions affected steelhead anglers more than any other group; since most Indian net fisheries were at the mouths of rivers, the tribes were in a position to take returning steelhead before anglers waiting upstream had a chance to fish for them.

The tribes were supposed to stop fishing when they had taken half the harvestable run, but because methods of calculating fish populations and spawning escapements are inherently imprecise, it sometimes happened that the Indians took more than half the harvestable fish, leaving sportsmen with little or nothing. Steelhead sport catches plummeted and many anglers scrawled angry or profane messages across their punch cards and sent them in. "Judge Boldt took all my fish" was one of the more common, and more polite, of these messages.

Non-Indian commercial fishermen also were hurt by the judge's decision. Many were stripped of a way of life they had always known—ironically, the same thing that happened to the Indians a century before—and they were bitter. They held protest marches, wrote angry letters to Congress, hung Judge Boldt in effigy, and some fished in defiance of the judge's orders and were sent to jail. Judge Boldt was a hero to the tribes and their supporters, but to nearly everyone else he was a target of violent hatred.

This was true even though an objective reading of his decision and the long, sorry history leading up to it could hardly fail to convince a reasonable person that the decision was both morally and legally correct (if not especially good for fisheries management). The trouble was that few people involved in the dispute were either objective or reasonable, and in his validation of Indian treaty rights Judge Boldt rekindled old prejudices and reopened old wounds that would best have been left forgotten.

The growing conflict and increasing violence following the decision prompted President Jimmy Carter to establish a task force to try to find a solution to the highly charged controversy. Representatives of Indian tribes, non-Indian commercial and sport-fishing groups and state fisheries-management agencies were invited to join negotiations aimed at finding an amicable settlement. As a representative of the state's fly-fishing clubs, I was given a seat at the table.

From the first meeting it was obvious there were enormous differences in the positions and perspectives of every interest group. Some non-Indian groups, convinced the Boldt decision would be overturned by the Supreme Court, probably were not even participating in good faith. Chances for a settlement appeared bleak.

But as long as there was even a small chance for agreement, some of us were determined to keep trying. During the next eighteen months I attended countless meetings and spent endless hours doing research or writing position papers and reports, all aimed at persuading bitter enemies and my own fly-fishing constituents that a compromise was in everyone's best interests.

It was a difficult, divisive time. Because I was willing to meet with tribal representatives, I was branded an "Indian lover" by some people I had once thought my friends. Emotion had clouded their judgment and some never spoke to me again.

But the negotiations continued and somehow, after many months, a settlement proposal was reached, one that offered benefits to each competing interest group. Steelhead anglers, including fly fishers, would regain some but not all of what they had lost under the Boldt decision, and I desperately hoped they would accept the proposal—if only on the grounds that half a loaf is better than none.

The proposal was made public with great fanfare and the task force called on the parent groups of all the negotiators to endorse it. This would be considered evidence of public support, which would give Congress the impetus needed to pass legislation implementing the agreement.

Days passed, then weeks, and the task force waited in vain. In the end not a single endorsement was forthcoming; the proposal died for want of a second. President Carter managed to achieve peace between Israel and Egypt, but he was not able to restore peaceful relations among rival fishing factions in the Pacific Northwest.

Despite the disappointing outcome, the experience taught me much about fish and fisheries management that I would never have learned otherwise; it also taught me a great deal about what makes fishermen tick. So I did not feel my efforts had been wasted.

The Supreme Court later upheld Judge Boldt's ruling and his restrictions on steelhead sport fishing became permanent. Anglers were left with only a fraction of the number of fish they had once been allowed to catch. Sales of steelhead-fishing licenses plummeted, and many who still bought licenses continued to vent their anger by scrawling "Judge Boldt took all my fish" on their punch cards.

The passage of years eventually dulled many of the passions ignited by the Boldt decision, but the familiar phrase "Judge Boldt took all my fish" was still very much on my mind when it came time to christen a new steelhead dry-fly pattern. The unnamed fly had obtained unusually good results, and I realized that over the seasons I had been fishing it, the pattern had accounted for nearly all the summer steelhead I had caught. It had taken all my fish.

What, then, could be more appropriate, or more deliciously ironic, than to name it after Judge Boldt?

So that's what I did, and that's why I did it.

Now, whenever I'm lucky enough to catch a summer steelhead and someone asks what fly I was using, I reply: "Judge Boldt takes all my fish."

THE JUDGE BOLDT IS EASY TO TIE. The first step is to cut a thin bunch of long, dark-brown deerhair and lay it atop the hook shank so the tips extend about a quarter of an inch beyond the bend; the tips will serve as the fly's tail. Tying thread is wound loosely over the hair; then a quick pull on the thread tightens the windings so the hair is bound evenly and firmly along the hook. This thin deerhair "underbody" adds buoyancy to the fly.

Next a larger bunch of deerhair is placed on the forward part of the hook with the tips extending beyond the eye. After the butts are bound firmly to the hook, the rest of the hair is pushed into an upright position to serve as the wing. Two or three turns of tying thread around the base of the wing help keep it in the upright position; a couple of turns of thread just forward of the hair also will help assure it stays in place. The butts of the hair should be trimmed as short as possible behind the spot where the hair was fastened to the hook.

When all this has been done, two thin strands of black nylon wool are tied in just behind the wing. These should be wound backward toward the rear of the fly, covering the deerhair "underbody" until the bend of the hook is reached; then the wool is wound back forward past its point of origin to a spot just in front of the wing. The wool is secured at that point and the excess trimmed away. The result should be a slim, uniformly shaped body.

The last step is to add the hackle. A feather of appropriate size should be taken from a high-quality natural black neck and its butt secured just forward of the wing. The hackle should be wound both fore and aft of the wing—this also will help keep the deerhair wing in position—then tied off in front of the wing and the excess trimmed away. After the head is finished and lacquer applied, the pattern is complete.

The Judge Boldt is designed to be fished with a riffle hitch, which is intended to keep the pull of the leader at an angle to the body of the fly. This angular pull, combined with the force of the river's current, keeps the fly afloat and allows it to create a highly visible wake as it swings around on a downstream cast. Most anglers believe this waking effect is what brings steelhead to the surface.

A riffle hitch is easy to tie. The fly is first tied to the leader in conventional fashion, then a pair of half hitches are taken to form a loop in the leader. The loop is slipped around the body of the fly and positioned at the point where you want the leader to pull on the fly; with most patterns this point is just in front of the wing; with the Judge Boldt, it is just *behind* the wing. Once the loop is positioned properly, pull gently on the leader to tighten the loop slowly around the body of the fly, taking care not to pinch down the hackle or the wing. When the loop is tight you're ready to go fishing.

Positioning the riffle hitch behind the wing of the Judge Boldt increases the angle of pull on the fly. This helps keep the fly on the surface in strong currents and creates a more visible wake.

The riffle hitch should always be tied so the leader comes off the side of the fly facing the angler; if it's on the other side, the leader will pull the fly under water instead of keeping it on top.

When I began fishing the Judge Boldt and other riffle-hitched patterns, I was in the habit of coating them heavily with silicone dressing in the mistaken belief this was necessary to keep them afloat. As a result, I always had a bunch of slightly used flies that looked as if they were having a bad hair day; they didn't float very well, either. Eventually I realized it was not necessary to apply dressing to a riffle-hitched fly; if the fly had been tied properly in the first place, if the riffle hitch was tied correctly, and if I maintained proper control of the line while fishing out each cast, the fly would stay afloat by itself.

I have been fishing riffle-hitched flies without dressing them ever since. If one becomes waterlogged and starts to sink in heavy water, I just clip it off, set it aside to dry, and replace it with a fresh fly.

THE FIRST REFERENCE IN MY ANGLING DIARY to the fly pattern that eventually became known as the Judge Boldt dates back more than twenty years. At the time I called the fly a "Giant Adams" because the prototype somewhat resembled the classic trout fly of that name. It had a gray dubbed fur body and mixed brown and grizzly hackle along with a deerhair wing and tail, and it accounted for the first steelhead I ever caught on a dry fly.

But I caught that fish in the middle of a sunny afternoon, and it seemed to me that for evening fishing a darker pattern would be more effective. So I tied a couple of flies with black wool bodies and black hackles and tried them late one muggy August evening when a fading blue glow on the western horizon was all that remained of the day. I started fishing at a favorite spot on the North Fork of the Stillaguamish known locally as "The Pocket." I had been fishing only about twenty minutes when a fish rose confidently to the unnamed black fly and took it solidly.

It was not a very spectacular fish, making only a single half-hearted jump and several short, sharp runs, and when it grudgingly followed me to the beach I saw it was a bright hen fish of only about four pounds, a typical native steelhead that appeared to be in far better condition than its fight indicated; perhaps it had been caught and released earlier by another angler. My riffle-hitched black fly was well back in the corner of her mouth, and I removed it quickly and returned the fish to the river, hoping she would go on to her spawning.

The next afternoon, fishing a different section of the river with the same black pattern, I had a quick rise as the riffle-hitched fly completed its swing. The fish ran strongly but then the line went slack, and when I reeled in and looked at the fly I saw the fine-wire hook had broken at the barb. I replaced the fly with another black pattern and rose and hooked another fish minutes later. This one ran quickly all the way into the backing, jumped repeatedly and fought the way summer steelhead are supposed to fight. I finally beached it at the tip of a little island, another hen fish, this one of hatchery origin—apparent from her ragged dorsal fin. I judged her weight about six pounds before I removed the fly and returned her to the river.

Over the next two days I landed two more steelhead, lost two others after long battles, and missed another rise—all on the same fly. It looked as if I'd found an effective pattern, not only for evening fishing but even for daylight hours. "Must think of a name for it," I wrote in my diary.

I did think of a couple of names for it, but quickly forgot them—which probably meant they weren't well suited for the pattern anyway. Mostly I just referred to it as "the nameless black pattern," or the "unnamed black fly," or "the riffle-hitched black pattern." But that was awkward, especially when somebody asked me what fly I'd been using, so I finally resolved to give the fly a proper name and stick with it.

I thought long and hard before I named it the Judge Boldt, for reasons already stated. The name seemed right, and I think it was—because it has stuck.

WHILE THE BLACK VERSION OF THE JUDGE BOLDT has proven most effective, there are several variations that also have taken their share of steelhead. One is the prototype I used to catch my first dry-fly steelhead, the "Giant Adams" version with gray dubbed fur body and mixed grizzly and brown hackle. Another version features a slim body of yellow wool with a light brown or ginger hackle. A third has a body of pink wool and light brown or ginger hackle. Yet another has a body of peacock herl with brown or mixed brown and grizzly hackle. All these variations are tied and fished the same way as the black Judge Boldt, and they seem to work best during daylight hours, especially on bright days. Though originally intended for evening fishing, the black version works well under all conditions.

The Judge Boldt is not the only dry fly I fish with a riffle hitch. I also like to use a Bomber pattern, originally developed for Atlantic salmon. The Bomber has a body of tightly packed clipped deerhair with dry-fly hackle palmered over its length, which makes it a very buoyant fly. This is good, because the thickness of its body means a riffle hitch can only be tied around the head of the fly, where the angle of pull is not very acute, but the fly's buoyancy helps compensate for this. The Bomber is an excellent exploratory fly, good for bringing steelhead to the surface but not very good at hooking them—at least in my experience. If I raise a steelhead to a Bomber and it fails to take, I usually switch to the Judge Boldt or one of its variants, and more often than not the fish will rise to the Judge Boldt and take it firmly.

But not always. The acute angle of pull on the riffle-hitched Judge Boldt sometimes makes it hard to set the hook solidly in a steelhead, and over the years I've lost many fish that were only lightly hooked. As they do often with a Bomber, steelhead also frequently rise to a Judge Boldt without actually taking it, just rolling next to the fly or sometimes bumping it with their noses without ever opening their mouths. This can be frustrating but also wildly exciting.

I suppose there are more effective methods of hooking steelhead and I would probably catch more if I resorted to some of them. But the sight of a steelhead rising to a dry fly is so spectacular that I wouldn't trade it for anything. Of course I'm disappointed if I lose or miss a fish, but I would rather have the memory of the rise than any other part of the experience.

THERE IS NO SUCH THING AS A "TYPICAL" FIGHT with a steelhead. Each fish is different, and sometimes both fish and fisherman behave unpredictably. Strange things happen.

One July evening I went out to fish the Elbow Hole near my cabin on the North Fork of the Stillaguamish. The sun had just left the water and the ambient light was still strong by the time I had fished my way down to a place where the current formed a crease over a submerged boulder. This, I knew, was a good spot, and I watched carefully as my riffle-hitched Judge Boldt sliced through the slick behind the boulder. Sure enough, a small steelhead rose and took the fly.

The fish jumped once, then started off on a run that made my reel chatter. Bob Headrick, my riverside neighbor, heard the sound of the reel and came to see what was happening. When he saw I was playing a fish, he yelled across the river to ask how large it was.

I had both hands busy just then, one on the rod, the other on the reel, so when I opened my mouth to respond to his question there was no free hand available to take the cigar I had forgotten I was smoking. The lighted cigar fell from my mouth and disappeared, and I was angry because I hadn't finished it yet.

But there was more important business at hand, so I turned my attention back to the fish and continued playing it—until suddenly I felt a very warm sensation inside my brand-new, very expensive Gore-Tex waders. The cigar had fallen inside the waders!

I don't now remember quite how I did it, but with one hand still on the rod and the fish still running, I used the other hand to grope around inside my waders—which by then were emitting smoke—until I found the cigar in the crotch of my trousers; fortunately it hadn't gone all the way down inside one of the wader legs. I withdrew the cigar, hurled it in the river and landed the fish—and only then checked to make certain the fire was out. Miraculously, the new waders weren't damaged, but there were some nasty scorch marks in the crotch of my jeans.

Thankfully, Bob had lost interest in my battle with the fish and returned to his house before I discovered the cigar in my crotch; otherwise he never would have let me live it down.

Even more thankfully, there was nobody around with a video camera.

SOMETIMES, BETWEEN FISHING SESSIONS ON THE NORTH FORK, I like to sit on the old wooden bench on the high bank overlooking the river and speculate about what I would have seen from the same vantage point two hundred years ago, before the first white men came to the valley.

There are some things I would *not* have seen: the open fields and the old barn on the far side of the river, the ragged clear-cuts that scar the nearby foothills, the steel skeletons of the radio towers on the mountains beyond the foothills. The towers were built to transmit launch orders to submerged missile submarines, and I suppose if there is ever a nuclear war they will be high on somebody's target list.

Two centuries ago nobody worried about such things.

Back then, the river would have been bordered on each bank by great ranks of ancient fir and cedar, disappearing into the winter mist or casting dark shade on the river during bright summer after-noons. Those huge trees would have dwarfed everything around them; even the river would have looked smaller than it does today. Now only a few trees stand watch over the river and all those are second-growth, having forced their way up through slash left by the loggers who passed this way in the late nineteenth or early twenti-eth century.

The loggers took everything. A few enormous stumps are all that remain of the grandeur that once existed here. Even after a century of rot, some are still large enough to defy imagination. They loom in the woods like the mysterious statues of Easter Island, mute evidence of a distant time. A few still show the places where loggers cut notches into them, platforms on which the sawyers stood to use giant handsaws for many hours until they had cut through the great tree that once grew from the stump.

Those trees shaded and protected the river, and as long as they stood along its banks the flow of the river was quick and clear and cold. Now, without the forest to provide shade and hold back runoff, the river swells quickly with spring runoff, then grows slow and warm and sluggish in late summer. Even then it often remains dirty with silt from savaged, tree-barren slopes.

Two centuries ago, before any of this happened, the river's channel would have been deeper and narrower than it is today. Silt from the logged-off slopes has filled the riverbed and raised its level so it can no longer handle the same volume of water it once did. Now it often floods in winter, causing great damage and sorrow.

If I could have seen the river two hundred years ago, I would have marveled at its incredible hatches of stoneflies, mayflies and caddisflies, much greater than the hatches I see today. There would also have been many more swallows, bats and nighthawks feeding on the great swarms of insects. All these creatures—insects, birds, bats— have suffered from removal of the forest and the subsequent siltation of the river. Now their numbers are but a small fraction of what they used to be.

Sadly, the same is true for fish. Two centuries ago the river had many more fish than it does now, a great many more. Back then it surely would not have been the work of a whole summer just to raise a few steelhead to a fly, as is the case now. The steelhead did manage to outlast the forest for at least a while; as recently as the 1950s, the native run was still large enough that it was rare for an angler to spend a day on the North Fork without hooking at least one or two steelhead. But the cumulative effects of logging finally caught up with the steelhead, too, and now those days are gone forever.

The coho salmon that once ran up the river so abundantly each fall suffered even more than the steelhead; now they are nearly extinct. Other salmon—chinook, pink and chum—still ascend the river, each in their own seasons, but their numbers, too, have greatly declined.

Indians fished the river two hundred years ago, as they still do today, but two centuries ago they did not fish with monofilament gillnets that kill indiscriminately and take many steelhead before any upstream angler has a chance to cast a fly over them. Yes, I remember: "Judge Boldt took all my fish."

Sitting there on my old wooden bench, looking down at the river and thinking about all this, it's easy to grow discouraged or depressed. But I have a certain cure for that: I go back to my cabin, get into my waders, pick up my fly rod, and head out on the river. The chances that I will hook a steelhead are infinitesimally smaller than they would have been two hundred years ago, or even fifty years ago, but there is still a small chance—and as long as any chance remains, I will keep fishing. And even if I should fail to see or hook a steelhead, the simple joy of fishing, the great variety of the river's sights and sounds, and the gentle feel of its current around my waist are enough to chase away gloomy thoughts of all that has been lost. Instead, I feel thankful for what remains.

And sometimes, every once in an increasingly great while, I'll find myself in just the right place at just the right time and a summer steelhead will rise spectacularly to my riffle-hitched fly.

You know which fly: Judge Boldt takes all my fish.

10

CUTTHROAT CANDY

Hook: No. 8 3X fine wire dry-fly hook
Tying thread: Tan or beige Monocord
Overlay or shellback: Brown deer body hair
Body: Tan or beige closed-cell foam
Hackle: Brown, palmered over length of body
Wing: Brown deer body hair (continuation of overlay, tied back to form wing)

SEATTLE OFTEN IS CALLED LATTÉ LAND, the coffee-quaffing capital of the world. The reputation is well deserved; there are espresso stands at nearly every major intersection, shopping mall and supermarket parking lot. Long lines of rain-soaked commuters form at these outlets every weekday morning, anxious for a hefty belt of caffeine to start the day.

So nobody was surprised when federal agencies took water samples and discovered the caffeine content of Puget Sound increases something like eight hundred percent between 8 and 8:30 every weekday morning. It could hardly be otherwise, given the thousands of bladders emptying hundreds of thousands of cups of coffee into the local sewer system. Neither the human digestive system nor the municipal sewage-treatment system has any effect on the caffeine, so it pours undiluted into Puget Sound with the same potency it had in each coffee cup.

The Environmental Protection Agency insists this giant daily caffeine jolt has no effect on the marine life of Puget Sound, but not everyone agrees. Some fly fishers, for example, think all that coffee is the main reason Puget Sound cutthroat fight the way they do: They're positively wired on caffeine.

They could be right. Imagine how you'd feel after fifteen or twenty cups of coffee. No wonder the fish jump like that.

IF YOU ASK ME, HOWEVER, the caffeine has nothing to do with it. I think sea-run cutthroat in Puget Sound have always fought that way, just because they are hard-nosed little fish, fish with chips on their shoulders.

And why not? The sea-run cutthroat doesn't receive anywhere as much attention or publicity as other fish that spend part of their lives in saltwater. The cutthroat isn't as glamorous as salmon or steelhead, it doesn't travel to the exotic destinations they do, and it doesn't grow nearly as large. Instead, it's just a stay-at-home fish that goes about its business privately and unobtrusively in the estuaries, a tough, hard-working, blue-collar kind of fish.

Or maybe blue collar is the wrong term. Perhaps blue blood would be better, because the cutthroat does one thing that scarcely any other fish in saltwater ever does: It rises willingly to a dry fly. And a fish that does that obviously belongs in the very best social circles.

I have written elsewhere of discovering that cutthroat would take dry flies in salt water and there's no need to repeat the details here. Suffice it to say that after years of stalking cutthroat, watching for their rises, then covering them with wet flies like the Tarboo Special, it dawned on me that these tactics made no sense. When a fish rises, you should cover it with a dry fly, not a wet fly.

So that's what I did, and it worked.

The fly I used for the experiment was a derivative of Lloyd Frese's Salmon Candy pattern. It had a thin body of brown nylon wool, brown hackle palmered over the length of the body, and a deerhair overlay and wing, both made from the same batch of hair. The hair was tied in at the bend of the hook, tips pointing backward, then brought forward over the top of the body and tied off behind the eye of the hook with tips pointing forward. The tips were then bent back to form a wing, which was secured by wrapping thread tightly over the spot where the hair was bent.

The pattern originally was meant to serve as an adult caddisfly imitation for use in fresh water and it worked well for that purpose, sometimes even superbly. A green-bodied version worked even better because most adult caddisflies I encountered had green bodies; those with brown bodies seemed fairly uncommon. But both green and brown versions of the fly shared one very important characteristic: They floated very well.

So when the time came to experiment with a dry fly in saltwater, I decided I needed a good, buoyant, high-floating pattern—one that could be skated across the surface like a freshwater traveling caddis—and the brown-bodied pattern seemed a good choice. Not only did it have the floating characteristics I was after, but I had also tied plenty of them and I wasn't using them for much of anything else.

When I tried it, the results were far better than I could have hoped, and I've been using the same pattern ever since. In fact, it is the only dry-fly pattern I use for sea-run cutthroat in saltwater.

FOR THE FIRST SEVERAL YEARS I FISHED THE CUTTHROAT CANDY, it didn't have a name. I still thought of it as a freshwater caddis pattern and noted it as such in my fishing diary, even when I used it to catch sea-run cutthroat in the estuaries. But as I began using the pattern more and more in saltwater and less and less as a caddis imitation, I realized it didn't make sense to keep calling it the latter. So I decided to give the fly a new name to reflect its predominant use.

I was still thinking about this when I went fishing on Hood Canal one soggy December day. It started raining just about the time I began fishing, as if the rain had been saving itself for my appearance, and it rained harder and harder as the day went on.

The fishing, however, was as good as the weather was bad. I hooked and landed a cutthroat on my very first cast and five more followed in quick succession. Four were typical sea-runs, no larger than twelve inches, but the two others were exceptional. One was a fat buck that gave me an unusually long run for a cutthroat and put up a good scrap from start to finish; it measured seventeen and one-half inches and was so thick and deep I judged its weight at close to three pounds. The other fought even harder and I could see it was a large fish, so I handled it delicately in consideration of the three-pound-test tippet I was using. After a long, dogged fight I finally led it to the boat and saw it was another buck, fat and hook-jawed. It measured twenty-one inches and I estimated its weight at four pounds. It still ranks as one of the largest cutthroat I've ever caught.

All six fish took the dry fly, and I wrote in my diary for the first time that the fly they had taken was the Cutthroat Candy. Considering it had been inspired by Lloyd Frese's Salmon Candy, the name seemed fitting.

The Cutthroat Candy has accounted for most of the sea-run cutthroat I've caught since I began using it, although I still use wet flies such as the Tarboo Special and Golden Shrimp when conditions indicate. In addition to cutthroat, the Candy also has taken several species of salmon, adult steelhead and sea-run Dolly Varden. It remains by far the most effective fly in my arsenal of estuary patterns.

NEARLY THREE DECADES HAVE PASSED SINCE I caught my first saltwater cutthroat on the Cutthroat Candy. During that time I have made several changes to the original pattern, all designed to increase its buoyancy.

The changes were dictated by the trout themselves. Sea-run cutthroat in saltwater sometimes will rise to a floating fly fished dead-drift, but they usually rise much more willingly to one skated over the surface. The original Cutthroat Candy, with the wool body, became waterlogged when skated repeatedly, and even generous applications of dry-fly dope were not enough to keep it floating. This was especially true in situations where the fly was being retrieved against the tide or wind, or sometimes both. The body would become waterlogged rapidly under those circumstances, and the deerhair overlay and wing simply did not provide enough buoyancy to keep the fly afloat.

In an effort to solve this problem, I abandoned the wool body and substituted one made of clipped deer hair. At the same time I eliminated the deerhair overlay and began tying in a separate deerhair wing. The resulting pattern—with clipped deerhair body, palmered brown hackle and short deerhair wing—did indeed have more buoyancy than the original, but it was also more difficult and time-consuming to tie. Still, that seemed an acceptable trade-off for a fly that floated better and could be fished longer than the original Cutthroat Candy.

For several years I tied the fly that way, but then I discovered the virtues of closed-cell foam. As its name implies, this stuff is full of tiny little hollow cells or bubbles, each full of air and each presumably "closed" so the air can't escape; this makes the foam naturally buoyant. It comes in several different forms, including thin sheets that can be cut into small strips suitable for body material. It's also available in a variety of colors.

So when I found sheets of beige or tan closed-cell foam, it gave me the idea that foam might offer a better alternative for the body of the Cutthroat Candy. A thin strip of foam could be wound onto the hook shank in the same manner as the brown wool used in the original pattern, except it would never become waterlogged and sink like the wool; instead, it would add to the fly's buoyancy.

The brown closed-cell foam worked beautifully, and now I've gone back to tying the fly the same way as the original, with a thin body, palmered brown hackle, deerhair overlay and wing. The only difference is that the body now is of foam instead of wool. The fly itself looks just as it did in the beginning.

Like its progenitor, the Salmon Candy, the Cutthroat Candy's deerhair overlay is vulnerable to the sharp teeth of mature trout. But this doesn't seem to be a problem with sea-run cutthroat; when they rise and take the fly, they typically turn away at a sharp angle so the hook usually lodges in the corner of their mouth where the deerhair overlay isn't subject to tooth damage. Only rarely does a sea-run tear up a fly badly enough that it has to be replaced.

But there is still one problem I have yet to solve, and that concerns the hook. As far as I have been able to determine, there is no such thing as a fine-wire stainless-steel hook, and the regular stainless-steel saltwater hooks are far too heavy to use for dry flies. For that reason, I have continued using bronzed fine-wire hooks made for use in fresh water. These hooks inevitably corrode after immersion in salt water, so they have a limited lifetime—which means I am constantly in need of more Cutthroat Candies.

THE NOTION THAT SEA-RUN CUTTHROAT could be caught on dry flies in saltwater took a while to catch on with other anglers. Ed Foss, my old fishing partner and the man who introduced me to sea-run fishing, was an ardent freshwater dry-fly angler but steadfastly refused to accept the idea that sea-run cutthroat would take dry flies in saltwater. Even when we fished together and he watched me land fish after fish on dry flies, he still insisted the dry fly had no place in estuary fishing.

"Those are only small fish you're catching," he would harrumph, even though the fish he was catching on wet flies were no larger.

Like most fly fishers, Ed was a traditionalist who believed in fishing the way he had been taught, and like every other sea-run cutthroat angler of his generation he had been taught to fish with wet flies. But he wasn't the only skeptic.

I had written an article about dry-fly fishing for sea-runs, presumptuously titled "The Dry Fly in Salt Water," and it was published in a national fly-fishing magazine. A well-known angling writer saw the article and telephoned to ask if I would take him fishing for sea-run cutthroat. He seemed more interested in the fish than the method I had described in the article, but that was of no matter.

I agreed to take him and when he arrived in town we went to one of my favorite spots on Hood Canal. We had been fishing only a short while when I hooked a sea-run and played it to the side of my boat.

"Keep it there until I can get a picture," he shouted, so I held the fish in the water next to my boat while he rowed within camera range. He focused his lens on the fish and saw the fly in its mouth.

"Hey, that's a dry fly!" he said incredulously.

"Sure it is," I said. "Didn't you read my article?"

"Of course I did, but I thought it was all just bullshit."

He learned otherwise that day. And so, gradually, did many other anglers.

Now dry-fly fishing for sea-run cutthroat in saltwater is common, and many anglers have developed their own patterns. Poppers also have become increasingly popular within the past few years. One proponent, Leland Miyawaki, has used poppers with success for salmon as well as cutthroat. He believes it's not the sound made by poppers that attracts the fish but rather the disturbance poppers make on the surface—an observation that dovetails with my own experience using the Cutthroat Candy.

I haven't joined the popper parade and probably won't, nor have I tried any of the new dry-fly patterns developed by other sea-run cutthroat anglers. I guess that's because, in my own way, I'm as much a traditionalist as my old friend Ed Foss. The Cutthroat Candy has always done the job and I've never seen any reason to change.

A GENERATION AGO, WHEN THE VALUE OF WILD FISH STOCKS was not as well understood or appreciated as it is now, efforts were made to augment cutthroat populations in the waters of Hood Canal and south Puget Sound by artificial means. These were stimulated by growing interest in the sea-run cutthroat as a sport fish, primarily among members of fly-fishing clubs. In response to the oft-expressed concerns of club members that some sea-run populations were in trouble, the state initiated a stocking and rearing program to supplement the native runs. Members of the Washington Fly Fishing Club and several others were invited to participate.

Club members were assigned the pleasant duty of capturing mature sea-run cutthroat that could be used as brood stock to provide eggs and fry for hatchery rearing. This, of course, meant the members had to go fishing for cutthroat in Puget Sound or Hood Canal, which they were more than happy to do. If they caught a mature or nearly mature cutthroat, they were supposed to place it in a live well to be held for transfer to a floating saltwater pen where it would be allowed to ripen for spawning.

In this manner cutthroat were obtained from several different locations, but once transferred into floating saltwater pens they confounded biologists by ripening at different times; this made it difficult to find males and females simultaneously ready for spawning. It also underscored how little was known about these fish; this was the first real evidence that sea-run populations in Puget Sound and Hood Canal were not all alike, as everyone had assumed, but actually included many distinct races of fish that spawned at different times. Unfortunately, little more has been learned about these fish in the years since.

Despite the difficulty of finding ripe pairs, enough eventually were found to produce a good crop of fertilized eggs. These were incubated until they hatched; when the hatchlings reached the alevin stage they were released into a state rearing pond where they would be fed until they grew to fingerling size.

At that point the state asked fly-fishing clubs to help mark the fish. Marking was necessary so after their release into saltwater the fish could be identified as of hatchery origin, giving fisheries managers a way to judge the success of the stocking program. The fish would be marked by removal of one pectoral fin.

On the appointed day, a group of Washington Fly Fishing Club members traveled to a state trout hatchery near the city of Puyallup where they joined members of several other fly-fishing clubs and everybody went to work clipping pectoral fins on 20,000 cutthroat fingerlings. The fish were slightly anesthetized, which made the task a little easier, but trying to hold a writhing three-inch cutthroat fingerling in your hand and snip off one of its pectoral fins is a challenge under any circumstances. Nevertheless, things went pretty smoothly until lunch time, when everybody took a break and several portable barbecues were fired up to grill hamburgers. Someone also had brought a couple of coolers full of beer, so in addition to a hamburger, nearly everybody had a beer or two. Or, in some cases, three.

Then everybody went back to work. If they had thought it was tough clipping pectoral fins on cutthroat fingerlings under ordinary circumstances, they found out very quickly that it was difficult or nearly impossible after two or three beers. It was an ugly scene, and the mortality rate of the fin-clipped fingerlings was a good deal higher than it should have been.

Nevertheless, enough fingerlings survived for the project to go forward, and when they reached smolting size they were transferred to a saltwater pen. When the fish were judged nearly ready for release into the waters of Puget Sound and Hood Canal, the state again called on local fly-fishing clubs to help mark the fish with numbered tags. This time there would be no beer.

So another contingent of Washington Fly Fishing Club members set out, traveling to the floating pens at Manchester on Puget Sound. Members lined up with tagging guns while cutthroat were dipped from pens and placed in a solution containing an anesthetic and antibiotic (to prevent infection from the wound made by insertion of the tag) and in a long day's work all the fish were tagged. This time the survival rate was high.

Shortly thereafter the fish were released. One batch of about five thousand cutthroat was liberated in Hood Canal, near one of the spots that Ed Foss and I liked to fish. We went there a couple of weeks later to sample the fishing.

An amazing sight greeted us. In a place where we had rarely seen another fisherman, dozens of people were lined up shoulder-to-shoulder on the beach, hurling spoons, gobs of bait and all manner of other contrivances into the water, where a huge school of splashing, rising cutthroat could be seen circling.

Even from the beach we could tell all the fish were wearing numbered tags. The five thousand cutthroat had remained right where they had been released two weeks earlier, and their presence was highly visible to anyone who cared to look—and it had drawn a crowd of opportunistic anglers.

Ed and I looked at one another. "What have we done?" he asked.

I didn't even want to contemplate the answer.

Since we were there, we decided to fish. I tied on a Cutthroat Candy and rose a fish on nearly every cast; after releasing forty cutthroat of uniform size, all wearing numbered tags, I was thoroughly bored and disgusted with the whole business. It was literally like shooting fish in a barrel.

Within a few weeks the beach anglers caught most of the five thousand cutthroat. Only a few survived to live as long as a year and most of those eventually were caught, still wearing their numbered tags. The same thing happened at other sites where fish were released.

These results convinced everybody that artificial rearing of sea-run cutthroat was a bad idea, so the program was abandoned. Now, years later, we understand that was the right decision for another good reason: If the hatchery program had continued, some of the hatchery-reared fish undoubtedly would have survived long enough to breed with their wild counterparts, compromising the genetic integrity of the native runs and threatening their future existence.

Those runs are now protected by catch-and-release regulations, which have allowed the populations to grow naturally. And that's the way it should be.

SOME DAYS EVEN THE MOST RELIABLE FLY fails to bring a fish. Sometimes, for reasons known only to them, the cutthroat are absent from their usual haunts—either that, or they are simply not in a mood to rise.

I remember one day when I anchored in shallow water off a favorite beach and started casting into the water near shore, hoping to intercept a cutthroat cruising along the cobbled bottom. I fished an hour without a touch and hadn't seen a sign of fish.

Then a small boy, about five or six years old, came running along the beach. He stopped and watched me for a little while and I waited for him to ask the Inevitable Question.

Finally he did: "Catch anything?"

"Not yet," I replied, with emphasis on the "yet," trying to convey a sense of optimism both to myself and the boy.

The boy thought about that for a moment, then spoke again. "I saw a big one jump right over there," he said, pointing to a spot about a hundred feet away.

"Oh? How long ago was that?" I asked.

"About a year ago."

At least he was trying to be helpful.

I took only one fish that day—and I didn't catch it where the little boy said he'd seen the big one jump.

Once I went fishing on Christmas Eve. Perhaps it was the spirit of the season, or maybe just something I had to drink, but for some reason I was inspired to record the day's events in verse. My fishing diary contains the following entry:

"This is the very first time, I do believe,
That I've ever gone fishing on Christmas Eve.

"The water was flat, the day cool and gray
As I started out fishing the first little bay

"For an hour or more not a fish did I see;
Then all of a sudden they were all around me

"To a dry fly they rose just as neat as you please;
Four cutthroat, two salmon, I landed with ease

"In three hours fishing that's surely not bad.
Then to Harold's Inn I went and a burger I had

"Which is where I am now, writing down this good stuff;
But I think maybe it's gone on long enough."

By day's end I had released eleven cutthroat, two silver salmon and a jack chinook. One of the cutthroat was a beautiful fish of about eighteen inches and two and three-quarter pounds, perfectly shaped and perfectly colored in shades of olive, silver and yellow. A nice Christmas present.

And all on the Cutthroat Candy.

11

GREEN MACHINE

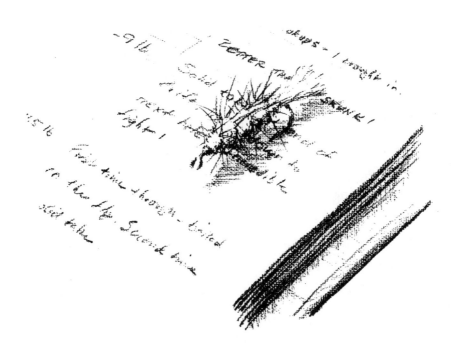

Hook: No. 8 or 10
Tying thread: Black
Tail (optional): White calftail
Tag: Fluorescent green floss
Body: Dyed green deer body hair, packed tightly and trimmed
Hackle: Brown, palmered over length of body

IF YOU SEARCH THE INTERNET FOR "Green Machine," you'll find entries for vacuum cleaners, an Australian football team ("Mal's Green Machine"), a "superbike" named the Green Machine, a brand of industrial street sweepers and a Los Angeles high-school debate team.

Keep looking, however, and eventually you'll start finding links to various fly-fishing web sites. That's because, as every Atlantic salmon fly fisher knows, the Green Machine isn't a vacuum cleaner, football team, bicycle, street sweeper or high-school debate team; it's an Atlantic salmon fly pattern—one of the best.

My acquaintance with the Green Machine started before my first trip to Salmon Brook Camp on New Brunswick's Main Southwest Miramichi. Howard Rossbach, my host at Salmon Brook, had told me the guides at the fishing camp considered the Green Machine the best fly—in fact, just about the only fly—to use on the Miramichi. He suggested it would be a good idea to tie some and take them along.

I looked up the pattern and saw I had all the necessary materials except the most important one, deerhair dyed emerald green, which I needed for the body. It took visits to several fly shops to find a patch of hair dyed the right color, but I finally found some and purchased it.

Deerhair may be the most difficult material for fly tyers to work with. It is hard to manage, flares in uncontrollable directions when cinched down on a hook, and is brittle and easy to break. But its naturally buoyant qualities also make it extremely useful in dry flies or other surface patterns, so most tyers are willing to put up with all the trouble, and some have become extraordinarily adept in working with deerhair.

Unfortunately, I'm not one of them. No matter how hard I try to pack hair tightly on the hook, my deerhair-bodied flies always end up with telltale gaps, like old dogs with mange. And no matter how valiantly I strive to trim the finished body evenly, it always turns out at least a little lopsided. For me, working with deerhair is about as much fun as shoveling fleas.

Nevertheless, I gave the Green Machine a good try, and tied a dozen in various sizes before I left for Salmon Brook. After I got there and met my guide, Charlie Munn, he asked to see the flies I had brought so I handed him the box containing the results of my efforts. He opened it, took a brief look inside, and handed it back. "Mebbe you better use one of mine," he said, opening his own fly box and taking out a Green Machine that easily put all mine to shame. I couldn't believe how firmly the deerhair was packed on the fly he gave me, or how its body was trimmed with perfect symmetry; whoever had tied this pattern was light years ahead of me.

I hooked my first two Atlantic salmon in the Miramichi on the Green Machine Charlie gave me. One was a big salmon I fought a long time and had almost to the beach when the fly pulled out. The other was a handsome nine-pounder that gave me a single long run and three spectacular jumps before it ended up in Charlie's net.

Charlie said he had purchased the fly at the famous W.W. Doak fly shop in nearby Doaktown, so at the first opportunity I went there to buy more. Like a kid in a candy store, I poured over the incredible fly displays; there were Green Machines with tails of white calftail, like the one I had been using, and others without tails, or with red butts. There were also scores of other patterns with deerhair bodies—Buck Bugs and Bombers in every size and color, Glitter Bugs, Rat-Faced MacDougalls, Wulff patterns and more.

Every one, it seemed, had a perfectly packed, perfectly trimmed, perfectly symmetrical deerhair body. I could have spent a fortune buying flies at Doak's, but with great exercise of will power I managed to limit myself to a dozen Green Machines in various sizes, plus a few other patterns.

Someone later told me there's a big difference between West Coast and East Coast deerhair; the former supposedly is coarse and more difficult to handle than the latter. I don't know if this is true, but hearing it made me feel a little better about my own abortive attempts to tie Green Machines; their scruffy appearance might have been due at least partly to my use of West Coast deerhair and not entirely to my own ineptitude. All the superbly tied patterns I had seen at Doak's fly shop were tied with hair from Eastern deer.

THE GREEN MACHINE IS NOT FISHED AS A DRY FLY but not quite as a wet fly, either. To a Miramichi guide, a dry fly is fished only one way, and that is upstream. It doesn't matter that the Green Machine stays on the surface; it is fished downstream, which in the guides' view makes it a wet fly. It is actually fished much the same way riffle-hitched flies are fished on Western steelhead rivers, with quartering downstream casts that allow the fly to swing around in a semicircle below the angler.

The Green Machine is tied to the leader tippet without a riffle hitch, but its buoyancy is so great that it sometimes behaves very much like a riffle-hitched pattern, kicking up a small wake as it swings across the surface. It may dip below the surface at the end of the swing, but most of the time it is on top or at least in the surface film. The local habit of calling it a wet fly is really just a matter of semantics; it's actually closer to a dry fly.

According to Jerry Doak, proprietor of Doak's fly shop, the Green Machine's origins can be traced to a Colorado angler. "An uncle of one of our most accomplished Miramichi guides had been in the employ of a brigadier general from Colorado in the early 1970s," Doak wrote in an article about the pattern. "During this time he accompanied (the general) on an excursion to the Eagle River in Labrador where he observed the use of an unidentified pattern fashioned from clipped green deer hair." The uncle "mentioned this to his nephew, Evelock Gilks, who, with a couple of other relatives, began to experiment with some green deerhair patterns on the Miramichi, based on variations of another popular clipped deerhair fly known as the Buck Bug."

Because white deerhair was in short supply, green dye was applied to brown deer body hair, which resulted in a dark olive color. This was used to tie the clipped body of a fly originally nicknamed the "Green Gobbler," which quickly proved its worth on the Miramichi. Word of the fly's success got around and others began copying the pattern, using different hair and dye combinations until the present emerald-green standard was established.

By the summer of 1980, the fly was selling extremely well at Doak's, even though it still didn't have a "proper" name. But a group of anglers who regularly fished the Mill Brook Pool at Nelson's Hollow near Doaktown were beginning to speak of a pattern they called the Green Machine, and upon investigation "we discovered they were referring to none other than this little green unidentified object," Jerry Doak wrote. "Thus it was that the little orphaned bug was finally given an identity"—the Green Machine.

Doak describes the Green Machine as an "austere, succinct, almost brutal example of fly tying at its most practical extreme. No passionate pursuit of plumage, no fondling of fur, no agonizing accuracy—just a bit of fluorescent green wool, a few sprigs of green deerhair, and a basic brown hackle are the only components for this most lethal of weapons. While its invention can hardly be termed an artistic achievement, it has, nonetheless, transformed many an uneventful day on many a river into something quite extraordinary indeed.

"In this dubious triumph of function over structure, the traditional complexities of fly tying are reduced to a level of simplicity that is more readily accessible to the ordinary individual. It is no surprise to find that for most people, a Green Machine is far less intimidating than a Green Highlander."

Easy for him to say.

Doak's article related how the Green Machine "began to emerge as a major force in salmon angling activities on the Miramichi and other rivers of Eastern Canada. With its catchy name and growing reputation, the Green Machine naturally received a great deal of enthusiastic attention, as well as no small amount of contempt and ridicule. Many a fisherman has categorically refused to stoop to the likes of a Green Machine, steadfastly resisting the urge to become caught up in all the hype and hoopla about this newfangled green thing. However, on rare occasions, when the fishing gets really tough, and fishermen get really desperate, principle sometimes gives way to expediency, and a 'Machine' or two is begrudgingly slipped into the fly box as a last resort."

That may have been the case in 1987, when Doak's article was written, but after several recent trips to the Miramichi I think it's safe to say the Green Machine is now the first fly anglers reach for on this river, not the last, and any hesitancy concerning its use has long since disappeared. Doak himself called it "the most productive fly on the Miramichi" and it's easy to see why; nearly everybody fishes it, and they undoubtedly fish it longer and harder than any other pattern. It's easy for a fly to be the most productive when it gets used more often than any other.

Certainly it has been the most productive fly I have used on the Miramichi.

BEFORE MY SECOND TRIP TO THE MIRAMICHI I tried tying more Green Machines, making every effort to get the deerhair tightly packed on the hook and the body neatly trimmed. The results were better than my first efforts, but still far short of Doak's perfection. Yet never having caught a fish in the Miramichi on a fly I tied myself, I was determined to try one of my own patterns.

The opportunity came one day when we were fishing from Charlie's canoe. I was in the bow and Charlie was seated behind me so he couldn't see what fly I was tying on, which gave me the chance to slip on one of my home-tied Green Machines.

I made perhaps a half dozen casts when Charlie said, "That fly's not tracking right. Mebbe I better have a look at it."

Wincing inwardly, I stripped in my line until Charlie could grasp the leader. He held up the fly and looked at it closely.

"Hmmpf," he said. "Mebbe you should use one of Doak's."

The fly had looked like it was tracking all right to me, but if Charlie had seen something wrong then I suppose the fish would have seen it, too. So I followed his advice, clipped off the fly and replaced it with one of Doak's.

And of course that was the pattern I was using when I saw a rising mound of water behind the fly and felt a slow, heavy take. As soon as it felt the hook, the fish leaped far out of the water, a beautiful, thick-bodied Atlantic salmon. Charlie quickly drove the canoe ashore and I hopped out, while the salmon took off for mid-river, running far into the backing and jumping repeatedly, a wonderful series of picturesque leaps. Twice more it ran and I was forced to follow along the shore until I was nearly one hundred and fifty yards downstream from the canoe.

After nine clean jumps and several more long runs, the fish finally tired and I led it to the beach. It weighed twelve pounds on Charlie's scale, although we both agreed it looked heavier. It was one of the prettiest fish I have ever seen, perfect in color and conformation, and Doak's perfectly tied Green Machine was planted proudly in the corner of its jaw.

Later that week Doak's Green Machines accounted for several grilse and two or three missed rises from other fish. I never did catch a fish on one of my own flies.

SINCE I BEGAN FISHING FOR ATLANTIC SALMON I have often been asked to compare them with steelhead. My angling experience is weighted so heavily toward the latter that I am probably not qualified to make such a comparison, but I would cautiously venture one observation: I think the steelhead is the more violent of the two.

A good steelhead, especially a prime summer fish, is totally unpredictable; it may run with unbelievable strength in any direction or jump repeatedly, and it may do either or both of these things with such incredible speed that an angler is left completely helpless during the opening moments of a fight. The steelhead burns energy at a furious rate and fights until utterly exhausted.

The Atlantic salmon, by contrast, is more graceful and deliberate in everything it does. It takes a fly more purposefully, without the wild, impulsive lunges a steelhead sometimes makes, and fights with a measured pace. A good early season salmon may run as far as a steelhead, or even farther, but without the same reckless violence. A salmon's leaps also are somehow more artistic and symmetrical than those of a steelhead, almost as if the fish were posing for a camera. A fresh salmon also fights with amazing endurance, drawing upon seemingly inexhaustible reserves of strength to prolong the contest.

You might say the Atlantic salmon fights by Marquis of Queensberry Rules while the steelhead is more of a back-alley brawler.

But having said all that, I don't think a comparison of the two is really very meaningful. Neither fish is better than the other; both are equally good, and each is superior in its own place, perfectly adapted to its environment from countless years of natural selection. Rather than trying to choose one over the other, we should be grateful nature has given us both. The best fish is always the one that happens to be on the end of your line, whether it's a steelhead in the Stillaguamish or an Atlantic salmon in the Miramichi.

There is, however, one marked difference between Atlantic salmon and steelhead—and that concerns their preference for the Green Machine. I've fished the Green Machine repeatedly (Doak's version as well as my own) for steelhead in my home water on the North Fork of the Stillaguamish. So far the fly has yet to raise a single fish.

I BELIEVE IT WOULD BE INSTRUCTIVE for West Coast fisheries managers and politicians to spend a little time in New Brunswick and see for themselves the many benefits that accrue from a well-managed river like the Main Southwest Miramichi.

Recognizing the economic worth of maintaining a world-class sport fishery, New Brunswick authorities now manage the Miramichi entirely for angling. Commercial netting was banned thirty years ago and the only fishing now permitted on the river is sport fishing with artificial flies. Non-resident anglers are required to fish with guides.

These regulations have improved both the fish and the fishing. Before the net ban, nearly all the adult salmon were taken by commercial fishermen and only smaller grilse got through the gauntlet of nets to enter the Miramichi system. Since netting was banned, the number of adult salmon entering the river has sometimes nearly rivaled the number of grilse. Current regulations even prohibit anglers from keeping adult salmon; only grilse may be kept, and these only in limited numbers. These rules assure mature salmon will survive to spawn; they also increase the odds that females will be fertilized by adult males instead of grilse. This in turn will select in favor of larger future runs of adult salmon.

The requirement that non-resident anglers must fish with guides provides many jobs during the salmon season—not just guiding jobs, but also numerous support jobs. Private ownership of much of the Main Southwest Miramichi has led to establishment of dozens of salmon camps and lodges, and each of these provides seasonal employment. True, these are not high-paying, year-round jobs, but in a perpetually less-than-prosperous area like New Brunswick they are extremely important to the local economy.

The quality of fishing available in the Miramichi also brings anglers from around the world, and in addition to the money they spend for guides and fishing-camp accommodations, they purchase gasoline, food, tackle, souvenirs and other items, and this pumps a great deal of money into the local economy, sustaining more jobs.

When all these things are added up, the total benefits are impressive—and they are responsible for a significant share of the economic activity in New Brunswick. Managing the river for sport fishing has thus worked well for everybody, bringing employment and wages to local residents and high-quality sport to visiting anglers.

If some of the best West Coast steelhead rivers were managed similarly, there is every reason to think they would provide similar benefits. Of course these waters are in public ownership, which precludes establishment of fishing camps or lodges on private water, but visiting anglers would still need local accommodations and this would mean more business for hotels, motels and restaurants. Persuading treaty Indian tribes to give up commercial steelhead fishing on rivers like the Stillaguamish would be difficult, but if the tribes were assured a fair share of the economic benefits they might be willing to go along. The result could be a net gain for everybody, as it has been in New Brunswick.

This is by no means a selfish proposal. It would surely mean increased angling pressure on any river under such management, and most of the best steelhead rivers already are crowded enough as it is. But if it meant better protection for the rivers, for fish habitat and for the fish themselves, it would be worth the trade-off.

Yet I don't expect anything like this will happen soon, if ever. Short-sighted politicians and their well-heeled friends in the timber and real-estate industries have always viewed the watersheds of steelhead rivers as places where all the trees should be cut and all the riverfront property should be "developed," and there's no reason to expect any immediate change in this myopic point of view. In fact, the very idea that portions of a few rivers should be managed under fly-fishing-only regulations is becoming an increasingly tough sell.

There are something like eight hundred rivers and eight thousand lakes in my home state of Washington, but those currently managed as fly-fishing-only waters represent less than one percent of the total. Yet the fly-only waters receive heavy use all season long, much heavier than waters not similarly regulated, which is proof in itself that more are needed. But there seems little prospect more will be established.

Politicians aren't entirely to blame for that. In recent years fly fishers themselves have been strangely reluctant to campaign for more fly-only waters, not only in the West but throughout the country. It's almost as if fly anglers have begun to believe what their opponents have always said of them: That they are an elite group, mostly wealthy doctors and lawyers undeserving of any special consideration. Instead of trying to refute that image, which is probably less true now than ever, many fly-fishing groups appear to have accepted it passively. Instead of pushing for more fly-fishing-only waters, as they once did, they have been all too willing to compromise and accept lesser restrictions, such as artificial lures only, reduced bag limits or catch-and-release.

These watered-down rules are certainly better than nothing, but they also fall well short of fly-fishing-only. And there is no reason fly fishers should feel compelled to accept such compromises when there is ample precedent for the dedication of public resources to single forms of recreation. Consider: Nearly every sizable community has public golf courses, tennis courts, swimming pools and similar amenities dedicated to single forms of recreation. All these occupy public lands, all were built with public funds, and all are maintained at public expense—yet they are reserved for relatively small groups of people. If you don't happen to play golf or tennis or swim, you are effectively banned from using these amenities.

Why should lakes and rivers be any different? If substantial public lands can be dedicated for the exclusive use of people who play golf, why shouldn't a few more public waters be dedicated for the exclusive use of people who fish only with flies? Fair play demands that they should.

But that's not the only reason. Fly fishers, especially those belonging to organized groups, tend to contribute more, financially and physically, to fisheries conservation and management than most other anglers, and they are entitled to a reasonable return on their investment. More fly-fishing-only waters would constitute a reasonable return.

Despite all this, management officials and politicians appear to have an almost psychological hang-up over the notion of dedicating a stream or lake to a single form of angling. Somehow it's much easier for people to accept the idea of taking public land and converting it to a golf course than taking a body of water and dedicating it to fly fishing. There's no good reason such a feeling should exist, but it does, and it will likely continue until fly fishers stand up on their wader-clad feet and begin to insist on their due.

I don't see that happening very soon. Perhaps the apathy that now seems to exist among fly fishers is due to a willingness to take advantage of the relatively few fly-fishing-only waters that already exist, such as the Main Southwest Miramichi. After all, it's always easier to accept the status quo than make an effort to change it.

So be thankful for waters like the Miramichi. We may not see many more of them.

ON MY LAST TRIP TO THE MIRAMICHI I arrived full of optimism. The river was in perfect shape and salmon were showing everywhere. It looked like the beginning of a perfect week.

The first evening I fished Salmon Brook Pool, the fishing camp's namesake, a spot where salmon often stop to rest in the cool water flowing in from the brook. The river felt right and I saw three fish jump in the pool while I was fishing it, all large salmon. But although I covered the pool thoroughly several times—first with a Green Machine, then an upstream Bomber, finally downstream with a wet fly—I never had a touch.

The next day brought heavy rain and the river looked as black as ink under a lowering sky. I fished four different pools, again with the Green Machine, the Bomber and a wet pattern, but never saw or touched a fish. A stormy sunset painted the river in shades of pastel pink and gold, but that was the day's only bright spot. When I returned to camp I learned that everyone else in the party had taken fish; I was the only one who so far had been blanked.

Next day was the Fourth of July. "Independence Day at Salmon Brook," I wrote in my diary; "independence for the fish, that is." More heavy rain had fallen overnight and it was still raining when we went out in the morning. Clouds were hanging in the treetops and the river was up several inches; not only that, but the water temperature had fallen several degrees, never a good thing for fishing in the Main Southwest Miramichi. Worse yet, the salmon we had seen upon arrival had disappeared, undoubtedly having moved upstream with the rise of water, and there was little evidence a fresh run had taken their place. What had started as such a promising week was beginning to look otherwise.

But I continued to fish hard. Drawing Murray's and Perley's Pools for the morning session, I gave each a thorough workout. The sight of a salmon leaping in the tail-out of Perley's brought momentary hope, but I couldn't coax it to my fly. A dark fish jumped out of the water in Murray's Pool, so close it made me even wetter than the rain that was continuing to fall. But nothing came to my fly except parr.

Meanwhile, despite the rapidly deteriorating conditions, Howard Rossbach took a grilse in the Black Rock Pool and his wife, Katie, lost one in the Salmon Brook Pool, leaving me feeling as if I had been stuck in the wrong place at the wrong time. We were nearly halfway through our week of fishing and not a single fish had come to my fly.

That evening the sky was dark and a humid fog shrouded the river. We had been fishing only a short time when nature obligingly provided Fourth of July fireworks with a spectacular display of lightning, bone-rattling thunder and hard, drenching rain. But those were the only fireworks, at least for me. The only salmon I saw was one I found lying dead among the rocks along the shore, a beautiful, bright, twelve-pounder without a mark on it. I wondered what had killed it—and if it was the only salmon I would see on this trip.

Next morning the rain had stopped, but the sky remained cloudy and a gale-force wind was blowing. Howling, shrieking gusts tore across the surface of the river and the rock maples along the riverbanks dipped and bowed dangerously. The river had risen even more overnight and the water temperature was down to an ominous sixty degrees, at least five degrees below what the guides considered a threshold for good fishing.

With only two days left to fish, I was beginning to feel snakebitten and resigned to going fishless. It wouldn't be the first time I had traveled a long way to get skunked, so I decided the best thing to do was try to swallow my disappointment, relax and enjoy the Miramichi fishing experience as much as I could.

I had drawn the Grilse Hole for the morning's fishing, and with Charlie poling the canoe and the wind gusting behind us we made the downstream trip in record time. The Grilse Hole had been the most productive spot all week, which gave me faint hope, but when we got there the wind was gusting so violently that the canoe's anchor chains kept dragging, making it impossible to hold position. Casting also was nearly impossible; I tried timing my casts between gusts, but the gusts came so frequently there was scarcely any interval between them. My line was blown into the water time after time.

Charlie struggled to maneuver the canoe so I could cover the best water, but the anchor chains kept dragging. I thought of the awful underwater racket the heavy chains must be making as they clattered over rocks and boulders on the river bottom; surely, if there were any fish in the pool, all that noise would put them off. But it didn't matter much; I couldn't get my fly over them properly anyway.

At length I suggested to Charlie that we might find a little shelter in Betts Pool, a short distance upstream. Betts was bordered by a steep, rocky cliff, and if we anchored in the lee of it we might escape the worst of the great, shuddering gusts that continued to sweep over the Grilse Hole. I had little expectation of finding fish in Betts—I had hooked a grilse there once, years before, but hadn't seen a fish in the pool since—but at least we might be able to keep the canoe in position and make a few decent casts.

Charlie agreed and poled us upriver, driving the canoe upstream with difficulty against the horrific wind. He anchored close to the face of the cliff, which did provide just enough shelter to keep the anchor chains from dragging and allow me to make some short, searching casts. With little hope, I began going through the repetitive motions of cast and retrieve, letting the fly sweep in short arcs along the wind-riffled water near the face of the cliff.

Then suddenly, unbelievably, I felt a strong take. I set the hook and Charlie lifted the anchor chains so he could put me ashore to fight the fish—but just at that moment a huge, screaming blast of wind hit us, the worst gust yet. The canoe rolled on its side and for an instant I thought we were going in, but with superhuman effort Charlie drove his spruce pole into the gravel and managed to right the canoe before we shipped any water.

The gust swept us away from the shelter of the cliff and far out across the river. Meanwhile the fish was running, peeling yards of line off my reel, but in the wild riverscape of blowing water I had no idea where it had gone, or how much line it had taken. All I could do was hold the rod high in a desperate bid to keep the fish from taking the line around a submerged rock.

Charlie tried to check the momentum of the rapidly moving canoe, throwing the anchor chains overboard and jabbing his pole repeatedly into the rocky bottom. The enormous gust that dislodged us from our original position finally blew itself out, but lesser gusts followed in its wake. Finally, several hundred yards downstream from where we had started, Charlie thrust his pole into the bottom and leaned on it with all his strength and managed to bring the careening canoe to a halt. That effort, combined with the weight of the anchor chains, held us in position long enough for me to recover some line and try to take control of the fight. I had seen the fish jump at least three times through the maelstrom of wind-driven water while we were drifting downstream, but still had no real idea of its size.

With the canoe's position stabilized, I was at last able to restore a tight connection to the fish. By then it appeared to have spent most of its strength, so I reeled in and brought it close to the canoe. Charlie abandoned his pole long enough to pick up the long-handled net and make a stab for the fish. He missed on the first and second tries but finally succeeded on the third; the mesh closed around the silvery flanks of what turned out to be a heavy grilse. I had hoped for a salmon, but it was not to be.

The grilse pulled Charlie's scale down to the five and one-half-pound mark and we admired it briefly before he slipped it back into the river. It turned out to be my only fish of the week, but it was enough to rescue me from the dismal ignominy of fishlessness.

The fly? A Green Machine, of course.

One of Doak's.

12

OTHER FAVORITES

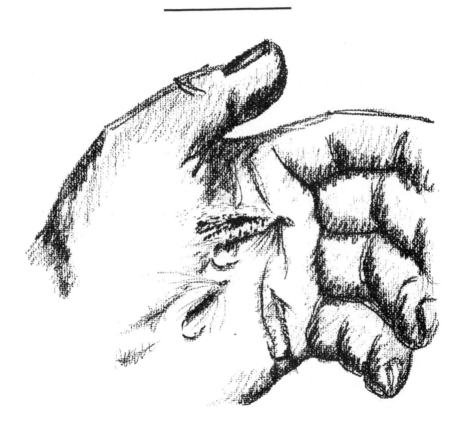

FLY FISHERS ARE FICKLE IN THEIR CHOICE OF PATTERNS. A fly that does the job one day may be forgotten the next, exchanged for another dressing that seems to work even better—yet the time will surely come when that fly, too, is discarded in favor of another that seems to offer even more promise. And so on and on.

At least that is how it has been in my fly-fishing life. In more than a half-century of angling I have enthusiastically embraced many patterns, used them for a time, then replaced them with something new or different. Yet not all the patterns that once did the job for me have been abandoned; I remain very fond of some and still carry them in my fly assortment even if I don't fish them very often any more. They have earned permanent places in my affections as well as my fly boxes.

The Black O'Lindsay is one such pattern. It was among the first flies I ever used, when I was still very young; I loved it then and I love it now. It is a handsome fly, a subtle blend of colors and textures pleasing to the eye and the touch, and I love it for that reason and for its beautifully alliterative name, which rolls so easily off the tongue.

As a boy, one of the things I liked about the Black O'Lindsay was that its name wasn't self-explanatory; it didn't have one of those dull, obvious names like "green nymph." The Black O'Lindsay wasn't even black, as its name seemed to imply, and to my young mind that somehow made it slightly mysterious—and as any small boy will tell you, fly patterns with slightly mysterious names always catch more fish than flies with common, boring, self-explanatory names.

Much later I learned the origin of the name and the mystery was solved. The Black O'Lindsay was the creation of Judge Spencer Black of Lindsay, California, a small town north of Bakersfield; the tyer's name and home town had been combined as the pattern's namesake. Judge Black had business interests that required him to travel often to British Columbia in the days before World War I and he combined business with pleasure by fishing during his visits to the province. The Black O'Lindsay, a wet fly, was his effort to imitate the grasshoppers common in the tall summer grass along the Walhachin reach of the Thompson River, where the judge often fished for trout.

The pattern gained local popularity, not just for Thompson River trout but also for steelhead in other British Columbia rivers and for Kamloops trout in the productive lakes of the province's southern interior. Long before the mid-1940s, when I began to accompany my father on fishing trips to British Columbia, the Black O'Lindsay had become a standard pattern among Kamloops trout fly fishers. It remained so for at least a quarter century.

Just why is a little difficult to explain. Certainly the Black O'Lindsay made a passable imitation of a drowned grasshopper when fished in the Thompson River, but grasshoppers are not ordinarily found on the Kamloops trout lakes, so the reason for the pattern's success in these waters is not readily apparent. But successful it surely was, and consistently so, or else it would not have remained a popular favorite so long.

Some anglers have speculated that the Black O'Lindsay imitates other natural foods found in the Kamloops trout lakes, such as dragonfly nymphs or, in smaller sizes, backswimmers. It's true the pattern does bear some resemblance in shape to a dragonfly nymph and some similarity in color to a backswimmer, but to consider it a good imitation of either would be something of a stretch. It also has been suggested that trout might take it as a caddis pupa, but this also seems unlikely. The Black O'Lindsay *does* make a reasonably good imitation of the giant water beetles found in some British Columbia lakes, but there are only a few lakes where these beetles are important as trout food, so this also fails to account for the fly's consistency as a fish-taker. More probably its success is due to the fact that it is a good "attractor" fly, possessed of some elusive quality that makes it appealing to trout even if it doesn't resemble anything a trout normally eats. That quality, and the fact that both anglers and trout were a good deal less sophisticated in Judge Black's day than they are now, may account for its success.

The Black O'Lindsay's use for steelhead—and also sometimes for sea-run cutthroat—never equalled its popularity as a Kamloops trout fly, although it enjoyed considerable longevity among British Columbia steelhead anglers. For the most part, it remains unknown outside the province.

The original pattern, as tied by Judge Black, appears to have been as follows:

BLACK O'LINDSAY

Hook: No. 6
Tying thread: Black
Tail: Dyed blue saddle hackle fibers
Body: Yellow wool, thick
Rib: Embossed gold tinsel
Throat: Dyed blue saddle hackle fibers
Hackle: Light brown, tied down as beard over throat
Wing: Barred mallard breast, parallel to hook, laid over eight strands of peacock sword

As with most popular fly patterns, the Black O'Lindsay inspired a number of variations. Most were not very significant, certainly not like the radical changes that have transformed other fly patterns into something completely different from their originators' intentions. Some tyers have substituted dyed yellow seal's fur for the body material, or tied the Black O'Lindsay with a full hackle instead of a beard. Others have used brown hackle for the tail and eliminated the blue throat altogether. A few have substituted black hackle for brown, and some (especially steelhead anglers) have added jungle-cock cheeks to the pattern.

Most of these changes appear to be the results of spur-of-the moment ideas, or the kind of thing that happens when a tyer discovers he lacks one of the ingredients of the original recipe and substitutes something else he has on hand, and few of these alternative dressings have taken hold. Unlike many fly patterns, the integrity of Judge Black's creation remains intact more than eighty years after it was born in his vise.

I SUPPOSE IT WAS MY FATHER WHO GAVE ME THE FIRST of the many Black O'Lindsays I have had. I used it to fish for Kamloops trout in Hihium Lake, British Columbia, at a time I was still considered too young to take a boat out on the lake myself. Instead, I went with my father or mother, and since I was also considered too young to master the rudiments of casting, one of them would row and I would troll the fly behind the boat on a sinking line.

If that sounds like a dull way of fishing, I would agree now that it is, but it seemed exciting then. Fishing was then still new and everything about it was exciting—the preparation, the travel, the sights, sounds and scents of unfamiliar country, and most of all the gleaming stretch of each new untried water. In my haste to make ready, I would invariably somehow get my line into an impossible tangle, or forget to soak the gut leaders we used then, or botch the knot that joined the leader to the fly.

Nothing ever happened quickly enough to suit me, and I couldn't understand why my father or his fishing partners would linger over breakfast or take their time getting things together in preparation for the day's fishing. Neither could I understand why they were reluctant to go out on days when it was raining, or a hard wind was blowing, or when the previous day's fishing had been dead slow. None of those things could dampen my spirits, and I was convinced that no matter how poor the conditions, each new day offered abundant opportunities.

Sometimes that childish optimism was fulfilled, especially at Hihium. In the mid-1940s that lake had many more trout than fishermen—sometimes I think the opposite is true now—and even a six-year-old dragging a fly behind a wooden boat was certain to hook his share. Years have dimmed some of the details, but not the memory of those throbbing pulls that came so quickly up the line, traveled down the slender bamboo shaft and entered my little hands like electric shocks. I remember anxious shouts of advice as I tried to strip in line while a trout careened wildly on the other end. Hihium trout seldom exceeded two or three pounds, but they were as strong and wild as any fish I've known, and if there was ever any doubt I would grow up to become a fishermen, those trout quickly dispelled it.

The Black O'Lindsay remained one of my favorite patterns well into adulthood and I fished it successfully on many other Kamloops trout waters. But as I gradually became more of a disciple of the doctrine of imitation, I found myself using the Black O'Lindsay less and less. I was not alone in this, for after a couple of generations of heavy use by Kamloops trout anglers, the Black O'Lindsay was beginning to give way rapidly to newer patterns that were both easier to tie and more careful imitations of specific trout foods.

Now the Black O'Lindsay is no longer in common usage, but I still carry at least a half dozen in various sizes among my selection of trout flies. Whenever I open that particular box, the sight of those flies never fails to trigger pleasant memories or revive my admiration for the beauty of the Black O'Lindsay and its alliterative name. And occasionally, when the newer imitations fail to work, I'll still tie on a Black O'Lindsay and stir up a reluctant trout or two. The Black O'Lindsay will always occupy an honored place in my fly box—and in my heart.

THE CAROT NYMPH WAS ANOTHER PATTERN I FISHED often as a young man. A simple pattern, sometimes also called "The Cutthroat's Delight," it was introduced to me by my old friend and mentor Enos Bradner, who also described it in his book, *Northwest Angling*:

"The Carot Nymph, an adaptation of Hardy's Partridge and Orange, has been another all-season fly for lowland lakes," Bradner wrote. "It will take rainbows and brook trout, but it is especially effective on native cutthroats when used in small lakes or beaver ponds on overcast or rainy days. Often the angler will raise a lunker cutthroat on a Carey Special but the trout will refuse to seize the lure. In such cases a stunt that often works is, instead of casting back, change to a No. 12 Carot Nymph. Then cast to the same spot and be ready to set the hook immediately, because the trout will usually hit as soon as the fly touches the water."

As Bradner noted, the Carot Nymph is an adaptation of an old British pattern called the Partridge and Orange, although not much of an adaptation. The gold tag is the only thing different from the original pattern; in all other respects it is the same fly. Bradner did not speculate on the origin of the fly's name, but I have a suspicion

it was named for its resemblance to a ripe carrot, probably by someone who couldn't spell very well.

The pattern:

CAROT NYMPH

Hook: No. 8-12

Tying thread: Black

Tag: Flat gold tinsel

Body: Orange floss, cigar-shaped

Hackle: Gray or brown partridge, tied "spider" fashion

Even as early as 1950, Bradner noted that the Hungarian partridge used for the hackle "has not been too plentiful in Washington
[State] and supplies of these skins are limited." That is even more
true today. But Bradner also correctly observed "it is certainly this
hackle feather that gives the fly its taking qualities. The . . . hackle
[should be] tied 'spider' [fashion] so that it spreads out like the ribs
of an umbrella. In the water, this nymph has the real movement that
gives it the appearance of a juicy morsel—a fit meal for any trout."
Today it would be classified a soft-hackle fly.

The Carot Nymph had a reputation for being a good beaver-
pond fly and it proved so for me. I used it often in the shaded little
ponds that were once abundant in the folds of the Cascade foothills.
Usually cluttered with drowned timber or submerged brush, these
were difficult places to fish, but they often held cutthroat or Eastern
brook trout, sometimes of impressive size. The Carot Nymph was
just bright enough to be easily visible in these wine-dark waters and
the seductive movement of its hackle was enough to persuade
almost any trout that here was, as Bradner put it, a "juicy morsel."

The Carot Nymph brought some fish that I still remember vividly. Once I was fishing a log-choked pond bordered by a steep cliff, a rampart whose rocky face was draped in veils of green moss and clusters of delicate fern. In the center was a lacy film of white water that plunged all the way from the clifftop to the surface of the pond. I admired the delicate beauty of the scene, but it also occurred to me the waterfall might bring food to trout waiting below, so I cast a Carot Nymph into the frothy spot where the waterfall met the pond. I let the fly sink a few seconds, then began a cautious retrieve. Almost instantly a fish grabbed the fly, and after a brisk fight I landed a cutthroat with some of the most beautiful markings I have ever seen on any fish, a blend of bright crimson, dark green and sparkling gold. It was the best fish I took that day.

Another time I went looking for a lake I had seen on a map. It turned out to be a far more difficult place to find than I had supposed, and I spent hours following faint trails through thick timber before I finally saw the glint of water up ahead. Emerging from the woods, I found myself on the shore of a fine, clear little lake. It looked deep in the middle but had shallow margins thick with underwater weed. A soft drizzle was falling, dimpling the surface, but here and there I could see larger disturbances where small trout were rising. There was no sign anyone else had been there in a long time, and it was serenely quiet.

On my second or third cast I felt the pull of a fish and quickly landed a small cutthroat. Within twenty minutes I had landed a dozen more, all plump, pan-sized, feisty little fish. They were marked with the same crimson, green and gold colors of the fish I had taken off the face of the cliff, with the added attraction of fins edged in bright gold. I continued fishing until I had released forty of these beautiful little trout, including a dozen that answered the call of a Carot Nymph.

The Carot Nymph was a good stream fly, too. Once I sampled a beaver pond that yielded only small trout, so I started fishing my way down the outlet, a fair-sized stream that grew steadily larger from the contributions of several small tributaries. Nothing came to my fly for a while, but then I drifted a No. 12 Carot Nymph under the roots of an old stump and had a furious answering pull. The size of the fish took me by surprise—I hadn't expected anything that large—and before I could react, it dashed quickly downstream under an old barbed-wire fence that stretched across the creek. The fish quickly tangled my leader around the lowest strand of barbed wire and broke off, taking the Carot Nymph along with it.

On my first trip with Ward McClure, who would become one of my regular fishing partners, we visited Williamson Creek, a tributary of the North Fork of the Sultan River northeast of Seattle. Using a floating line and a Carot Nymph, I fished upstream and captured four nice rainbows from a single pool. It was intensely interesting fishing, requiring a watchful eye on the floating line as it drifted downstream in the current, then striking at the least hesitation of the line—usually to find a trout on the other end.

That was long ago and that stretch of Williamson Creek is now submerged under the waters of a reservoir. Many of the beaver ponds I once fished have similarly vanished, victims of logging, sprawling real-estate developments, highway projects, or other infringements of modern civilization.

Since I used the Carot Nymph primarily as a beaver-pond fly, the loss of so many such waters has meant fewer places to fish the pattern. That, plus the fact that it never imitated anything in particular, finally led me to stop using it. But remembering all the fish it caught for me in years past, I still carry a few Carot Nymphs whenever I go fishing for trout. I haven't used it lately, but I have no doubt the time will come, perhaps soon, when I will want to use it again—if other patterns fail or if fate should happen to lead me to a beaver pond still hidden from the destructive forces of modern civilization.

TRYING TO COME UP WITH A REALISTIC IMITATION of the damselfly nymph is perhaps the most difficult problem faced by stillwater fly fishers. Damselflies hatch in nearly all lakes in the Cascade rainshadow, usually early in June depending on the elevation, and when the damsel emergence is fully under way the trout key on the nymphs to the exclusion of just about everything else.

Fly tyers long ago figured out how to imitate the appearance of the nymph, but even the very best tyers have yet to come up with a way of imitating its seductive wiggle. And that's the problem, because even a deadly looking imitation has little chance of success if it can't match the sinuous sidewinder movements of the natural.

My first attempt to imitate a damselfly nymph still ranks as my best, although I readily admit it leaves much to be desired. I had caught a trout with damselfly nymphs in its stomach and mounted a vise on the seat of my boat so I could try to make a copy of the natural. The result definitely resembled a damselfly nymph, or at least I thought it did, and showed immediate promise by taking several trout the first time I used it. I fished it with at least moderate success in many waters and eventually it became the first (and still only) fly to bring me more than a hundred fish in one day, although these were Eastern brook trout, or char, which everybody knows are not as wise or sophisticated as rainbow or brown trout. Even on that memorable day, the damselfly nymph emergence was fairly sparse; if it had been heavy I probably would not have caught as many fish, for by then I had learned that when the damselfly hatch is at its peak, trout—even brook trout—grow unbelievably selective and refuse anything that doesn't match the strip-tease movements of the real thing.

In company with many other tyers, I've spent a lot of time and effort trying to come up with a way to imitate this seductive motion. I've tried patterns with marabou tails, which should have wiggled in a lifelike manner in the water, but didn't. I've tried patterns with a combination of marabou tail and buoyant deerhair wingcase, the latter intended to keep the fly near the surface film where the naturals swim, but that combination didn't work either. I've tried slightly weighted patterns, also with marabou tails, in the hope that if the fly sank between pulls of the retrieve, the tail might wiggle seductively—but it didn't. Each of these experiments took a few suicidal trout, but when the hatch got heavy the patterns became virtually useless.

Flies with bodies of brown or olive-dyed pheasant rump, similar to the "Self-Bodied" Carey Special, looked good in the hand but were pretty much lifeless in the water. A pattern with an extended body of dyed green mallard breast seemed to offer great promise, but I couldn't keep it from spinning in the air when cast or in the water when retrieved, and the leader became hopelessly twisted.

I tried using "Microfibbets"—thin plastic strips intended for tails in mayfly patterns—bound together with epoxy in the shape of a damselfly nymph body. The result looked real enough but proved lifeless in the water.

I tried adding small plastic eyes to many of these same patterns, hoping a little added touch of realism might spell the difference—

but it didn't. It was the slinky motion of the natural the trout cared about, not the eyes.

A friend gave me an experimental pattern tied on a small hook with a clever wire hinge at the back; the rear portion of the fly's body was attached to the hinge so it could swing back and forth in the water. Good idea, but it didn't work either; when the fly was retrieved, the pull was straight ahead so there was nothing to cause the rear end to swing back and forth.

With each successive failure I was inspired to return to my original pattern, which continued to work a little better than all the others—although still not nearly as well as I thought it should. Like all the others, it was most effective at the very beginning of a hatch when only a few damselfly nymphs were present but became steadily less effective as the number of naturals increased. It did help some to fish the pattern with a riffle hitch; the angular pull of the riffle-hitched leader on the fly caused it to weave back and forth in the water, but never as seductively as the real thing. It acted like a damselfly nymph with severe lower-back problems, and not many trout were fooled.

So it is with some hesitancy that I offer the pattern. By no means does it represent the final answer to the damselfly problem, just the best answer that I have so far been able to devise. Consider it a work in progress:

DAMSELFLY NYMPH

Hook: No. 10 3XL
Tying thread: Olive silk or Monocord
Tail: Two dyed olive saddle hackle tips

Body: Light green chenille, thin
Overlay: Single strand of dark olive chenille placed atop body and bound in place by ribbing
Ribbing: Tying thread
Thorax: Light green chenille (same as used for body), built up so diameter is larger than body
Wingcase: Pheasant rump hackle dyed olive green
Legs: Several long fibers from wingcase, divided and tied back on both sides of hook

This pattern is darker on the back (dorsal) side than on the belly, which is true of many naturals. For best results, it should be fished with a riffle hitch.

After years of working on the damselfly nymph puzzle, I have come to the conclusion that it will probably never be completely solved. But if I'm wrong, and somebody finally succeeds in crafting a fly that imitates the motion of the swimming natural, he or she will surely deserve the thanks of legions of frustrated fly tyers.

I HAVE BEEN WELL SERVED BY MANY OTHER fly patterns over the years. Soon after I began tying my own flies I created a nondescript little nymph pattern that seemed to catch trout wherever I used it. It was a simple little thing with a body and thorax of tan floss, a rib of black tying silk, and a brown pheasant wingcase, all tied on a No. 12 hook. It resembled nothing in nature but seemed to have a look that trout found appealing.

These were mostly very unsophisticated trout, however, and I was then still a very unsophisticated angler, and the nymph pattern—which I had presumptively named the "Reliable"—didn't work as well when I began using it in hard-fished waters where trout were wiser. Also, as I learned more about aquatic entomology and became more interested in the science of imitation, I became increasingly bothered that my nymph pattern didn't really imitate anything. So I began fishing it less often and now rarely fish it at all. But I tied so many when I was young that I still have a good supply of them in my portable "filing cabinet" of flies.

Another invention, called the Northern Light, enjoyed brief success. It was the simplest of flies, just a shank of dyed hot-pink calf-tail lashed to a hook, intended to imitate the long, thin, crimson Chironomid larva known popularly as the bloodworm. It was a dynamite fly for a couple of seasons—I remember once catching seven four-pound rainbows in a row on this pattern—but then, for reasons I have never been able to fathom, it suddenly seemed to lose its effectiveness. I still have a few in one of my fly boxes, but their colors have faded so badly I don't know why I bother to keep them.

The Dr. Spratley is an old British Columbia stillwater pattern that I have used since childhood and still use occasionally with good results in British Columbia lakes. The Dead Chicken, a fly almost as ugly as its name, was a favorite when I started fishing for sea-run cutthroat, but I lost the last one I had several years ago. Knudson's Spider was another pattern I used then and still use now, but I use it today mostly for Pacific salmon instead of sea-runs. It's another very simple fly—just a chenille body and a very full hackle of barred mallard breast—but I have changed the body color from the yellow used by Al Knudson, the fly's originator, to chartreuse, which seems more appealing to salmon.

On one of my trips to New Zealand I acquired a pattern (or "lure," as the Kiwis call it) known as Hamill's Killer, and I have found it occasionally effective as a dragonfly nymph imitation in

North American waters. I also still have great confidence in my son Randy's steelhead pattern, the Retiary. I now use it most often in estuaries, where it works for sea-run cutthroat and other species besides steelhead, and it can be devastatingly effective.

I could go on, for there are many other patterns I have used with good effect for a day, a week, a season, or for many seasons. By now, however, you are probably wondering if I ever fish with the famous patterns all fly fishers know—the Muddler Minnow, Adams, Royal Coachman, and so on. The answer, of course, is yes; I have caught fish on all these and many others equally famous, and I expect to catch more. But given the choice, I would much rather fish one of my own creations, or at least one of my variations on a standard theme. I also find endless pleasure in experimenting with new patterns and derive enormous satisfaction when one succeeds.

Of course it's not always practical to fish your own patterns. Sometimes someone else has already created a fly that does the job about as well as it can be done, and it just makes good sense to take advantage of their work. Some of the flies in this book—the Carey Special, Crazy Charlie, Green Machine and Skunk—are such examples. These patterns have won my respect and confidence; they work so well there is little point trying to come up with something better.

And yet . . . and yet, whenever time and circumstances permit, I would rather use patterns that are the products of my own mind's eye, my own imagination, my own experience. My flies may never be worth framing and hanging on the wall, but as long as the fish are willing to take them, I will be satisfied.

IT'S OFTEN SAID THERE'S LITTLE NEW IN FLY TYING. There are only so many ways materials can be applied to a hook and most, if not all, have already been discovered. The "new" fly patterns that constantly appear in the magazines are usually just variations of older dressings or recycled ideas or techniques. Fly tyers, it seems, have already invented just about everything fishermen need. But that doesn't stop people from trying to come up with new patterns, or at least patterns they *think* are new, and there will never be an end to the number of dressings on the market.

Why are there so many? Why can't tyers leave established patterns alone? Why must they keep tinkering with them, trying different materials, different colors, different tying techniques? Why can't they accept the reality that little is really new in fly tying?

The reason is the same one that keeps me tinkering with established patterns and trying to create new ones of my own: Each tyer has his own unique view of the world. A caddisfly adult or swimming mayfly nymph is unique in the eye of each beholder, and it's human nature for each tyer to try to replicate it in his own way. Except for the boundaries of imagination, there are no limits to this process. It keeps us all striving for our own version of the truth, and while there may be little that is new in fly tying, we can still achieve results that are new to each of *us*. And that's what counts.

I believe fly tyers, like fishermen, go through a sort of personal metamorphosis. They start by tying only established patterns, usually the most simple flies first, then gradually work their way up to patterns requiring more difficult techniques, learning the skills needed to advance to the next level. This comes when they grow tired of following established recipes and begin experimenting on their own, convinced, as human nature dictates they must be, that they can improve on whatever has gone before. Sometimes they succeed; more often they do not.

Eventually most tyers reach a point where they realize knowledge of entomology is a prerequisite to further advance, so they begin to study and learn about aquatic insects, then strive to fashion imitations of the insects they have studied or observed. In doing so, each tyer again brings his own personal touch of creativity to the vise.

A few tyers advance even further, to the ultimate stage in which their work becomes art. The goal of imitation is often abandoned in favor of artistic perfection, and a tyer may labor many hours to fashion a single fly—perhaps a classic Atlantic salmon pattern incorporating a multitude of rare and delicate materials. The results are flies never intended to be fished; instead they are feasts for the eye, works of art to be prized as much as a rare first edition or a painting by a master.

And that's why there are so many fly patterns: Each tyer, at each level, sees things his own way and follows his own instincts and imagination. The result is an infinite number of combinations and permutations, which leads to an infinite number of fly patterns.

Sometimes—rarely—someone creates a pattern that works so well other fishermen are willing to accept it as even better than their own. These discoveries give us the universal favorites—the Muddlers, the Adamses, the Coachmen, and so on. Few flies ever achieve such popularity, however, and of the many thousands of established patterns, most remain obscure, fished only by a few.

But that will never stop fly tyers from trying to create more.

All this is as it should be. Fly tying, at its most fundamental level, is a form of human creativity. Like art and music, it has its share of romanticists and impressionists, realists and abstractionists. The vise is their easel, and their canvas is as broad as the universe.

Flies represent life. For most of us, however, they are also a vital *part* of life.